Sex and Sacredness

CHRISTOPHER DERRICK

'Sex and Sacredness,

A Catholic Homage to Venus

IGNATIUS PRESS   SAN FRANCISCO

With ecclesiastical approval
© Ignatius Press 1982
All rights reserved
ISBN 0–89870–018–3
Library of Congress Catalogue number 82–80302
Printed in the United States of America

TO CHAUNCEY STILLMAN

On ne badine pas avec l'amour

Contents

Introduction

Our world is short of various things, but it is not short of
books about sex. There must be thousands of them,
available on every side. Do we need any more? Apart
from various developing fields of specialist research, is it
possible to say anything about sex that hasn't been said a
million times already? Yet the books keep on appearing:
it seems that we can't stop talking about sex, whether we
have anything to say about it or not. Despite its inherent
interest, the subject is in some danger of becoming a
bore.

Any new book about it therefore needs to justify its
existence, to specify its point and purpose and the scope
of any originality that it claims. This present book is no
exception.

I offer it with a twofold purpose in mind.

It is intended, firstly, to promote mutual understanding in an area that is at present marked by mutual
incomprehension or bewilderment. I do not suppose
that I can bring the two sides to agreement. But I think I
can help to clarify the issue between them, so bringing
each side to a better understanding of what the other side
is trying to say.

In a matter so large and complicated as sex, it is of
course an oversimplification to speak of two neatly-
opposed 'sides'. The scope of this book is therefore
specialised and selective: it does not propose an overall

philosophy of sex, with all questions answered. But I
consider it clear that within the larger picture, what I
have called two 'sides' do exist and are at cross-purposes
rather than in simple disagreement. Both sides talk about
sex. But they talk about it in such different terms that
they almost appear to be talking about two different
subjects. They differ clearly enough in their conclusions,
their practical recommendations. But they do so by
reason of a more profound disagreement: they start off
from radically different preconceptions about what sex
is, and the trouble is that those two different preconceptions are often held unconsciously. Hence the cross-
purposes, the mutual incomprehension or bewilderment
that I have mentioned. If I can ease this by bringing their
more radical disagreement into the daylight, I shall have
achieved my primary purpose.

Each of the two 'sides' that I have mentioned is a
complex thing. In order to indicate very broadly what I
have in mind, I might point at a strict Catholic morality
of sex on the one hand, and on the other, at what we
loosely call the 'permissive society'. A more specific
instance might be provided by the moral question of
contraception. All the world knows that this has been regarded as inherently sinful within the Catholic tradition:
Pope Paul VI reaffirmed that judgment most solemnly in
1968, and Pope John Paul II has endorsed it repeatedly. A
great many people disagree, some Catholics included:
they maintain that in certain circumstances at least, contraception can be wholly innocent and even perhaps a
moral duty. So far, we are talking about a square and
simple disagreement. But we should note that mutual
bewilderment is involved as well. On the one side, it
might be expressed in such words as these: "What on

earth is the Pope talking about? What's *wrong* with contraception, for heaven's sake? It doesn't hurt anybody, it is done in private and doesn't offend public decency: it eases various well-known kinds of stress and so makes for human happiness: in a crowded world, it might be regarded as a moral duty. If the Pill has dangerous side-effects, that's a question for the doctors. But why should contraception, as such, be regarded as raising moral issues *at all*? What has it got to do with the Church?" Such things are often said: we may need to remember that there can be an exactly similar bewilderment on the other side. "What has happened to the world? We naturally expect mere hedonists to speak in the language of mere hedonism. But how *can* Christian people, ministers and priests included, justify so lewd a perversion? How *can* they encourage loving couples to behave in a manner hitherto deemed suitable for prostitutes alone?"

This particular question has recently acquired an almost obsessive kind of topicality: all present-day debate about Catholicism tends to recur constantly to the encyclical *Humanae Vitae*, as though little else in a complex and challenging Faith were comparably interesting and irritating to the modern mind. This sometimes appears to be the prime point of tension between the Church and the world; and I shall be betraying no domestic secrets when I say that it generates similar tensions within the Church.

But this is only one particularly sensitive point within a wider confrontation. It isn't only the Pope and the Catholics whom we find on the one side, and it isn't only contraception that generates that kind of mutual bewilderment. We speak too simply of a 'permissive

society': we should note—perhaps in some perplexity—
that those who are permissive about sex are often highly
moralistic about other matters—about social and military questions, for example. They, on their side, are
perplexed as well. *Why* should so many Christians, and
others as well, cling so obstinately to a set of archaic
and arbitrary taboos about 'fornication' and 'adultery'
and 'perversion' and all those other hobgoblins? Can
it be that Christianity was hostile to sexuality and the
flesh from the very beginning, and that the consequent
hang-ups and neuroses are still influential, even in the
minds of some unbelievers? "No!" reply the Christians.
"We have always said that sex was made and intended by
God and is a good thing!" "Then why have you always
been so negative and suspicious about it in practice?"

So the argument continues. In all the complexity of
our sexual attitudes, there is this fairly clear-cut phenomenon of two 'sides', in the sense of two moral codes.
Each is self-consistent and is held and followed by many,
and each arouses not merely disagreement but perplexity
in those who hold the other. How *can* people, otherwise
sensible and decent and well-meaning, think and behave
like that? What kind of psychological or other mess are
they in?

It is this mutual perplexity that I hope to ease. What I
propose is a kind of experiment. What will happen if we
lift this entire subject out of its normal home, which lies
in the realm of ethics or morality, and transfer it bodily
into the deeper realm of 'religion'? What will happen if
we consider it in relation to the concept of 'sacredness'?

Note that for the purposes of this experiment, I use
each of those two words in the broadest possible sense. I
speak of 'religion' as found among pagans and primitives

no less than among Catholic Christians: I use the word 'sacredness', not precisely in the sense it bears within the present-day Catholic vocabulary, but in the rather different and more double-edged sense that it has for the student of comparative religion—the sense that was explored by Mircea Eliade and Rudolf Otto among others. I write as a Catholic but mostly in pre-Christian terms; and in so doing, I follow the old principle that Catholic teaching about sex lies mostly within the field of 'natural law', however 'unnatural' it may seem to some. I thus find it lawful and convenient to use the name of a pagan goddess, just as though 'Venus' really existed and was really divine. Let the devout be re-assured: I intend no actual polytheism, no idolatry. Nor, despite some possibly shocking observations in Chapter III and elsewhere, have I any desire to bring the blush of shame to the cheek of modesty.

Note also that my experiment will be a strictly temporary one. If I transfer this subject of sex from the realm of morality to the realm of religion, this does not mean that I want to eliminate the concept of sexual morality, or play it down, or modify the ancient rules. I offer nothing but a perspective—one in which a mutually baffling disagreement about sexual behaviour will (I believe) be revealed as a fairly straightforward disagreement about Venus and her divinity.

This brings me to my second purpose in writing.

It is generally agreed that we have recently lived through something of a 'sexual revolution': my two 'sides' can be more or less defined in terms of friendly and hostile attitudes towards this. Its roots lie back in the nineteenth century: its first major development was in the 1920s, and it has achieved a kind of consummation in the decades since the Second World War. It may or may not go yet further: some claim to see signs of a substantial counter-revolution, and it is certainly no rare thing to meet young people who are in revolt against the sexual 'permissiveness' of the day. But so far, the revolutionaries have mostly had their way.

But about the interpretation of their cause, there can be different opinions. As with any revolution, a kind of official orthodoxy tells us to see this as the cause of mere freedom, of liberation; and as regards the social and legal controls upon our sexual behaviour, there is some obvious truth in this.

But is that the whole story? I see such matters from the rather specialised angle of a literary critic who is also a religious controversialist; and in each of these capacities, I have seen much to suggest that the real driving force behind this revolution was something deeper and more questionable than any simple desire for freedom and pleasure and fulfilment. That desire was present and powerful. But behind it, I have long seen evidence of a revolutionary hatred for Venus herself, as for some proud King or Emperor who had oppressed the people for too long and needed to be dethroned and cut down to size. It seems to me that the secular culture of our time is characterised by an all-pervading hatred and fear of sex.

I wanted to speak up in the opposite sense: as a thinly-baptised pagan, I wanted to speak up for Venus in all her glory, and against those who would desacralise her into something trivial or worse. It was in a real but secondary way that I wanted to do so as a Catholic. The Roman Synod of 1980 called for a deeper study of Catholic teaching about sex, with special reference to contraception: if this book goes some way towards meeting the wishes of the Synod, I shall be glad enough. But I would hate it to be supposed that I write solely—or chiefly, or at all—as an act of ecclesiastical obedience. It is mostly for long-term personal reasons, rooted in my experience as well as in my reading, that I here develop certain earlier lines of thought and so offer Venus this defence, this argumentative act of homage and reparation. I venerate her, I love her; and I intensely dislike this present-day habit of treating her with indifference or contempt.

It may seem paradoxical to suggest that Venus is seen contemptuously in the modern secular culture and has few friends or champions outside a fully traditional Catholicism. I hope to show that the paradox is only apparent and superficial. In the meantime, I would beg the sceptical reader to reflect upon political experience. Every revolution speaks of liberation and brotherhood and love. But the real force behind it will usually be different. The fine talk deceives some people. But what fuels revolution is the destructive power of hate.

This is an essay, not a work of scholarship: it might even be called a set of variously-angled meditations upon a single theme. Let no reader make false inferences from the fact that its pages echo with the patter of tiny footnotes. The function of these is seldom more than illustrative: close attention to them will make my academic limitations sufficiently clear.

They hardly matter for the purpose I have in mind. The relevant facts have already been discovered by others and are not (I believe) seriously in dispute. My experiment is simply a matter of re-arranging them in a possibly unfamiliar way, so as to cast new light upon a familiar subject. It is in that respect alone that I claim a certain originality and justification for this book.

Chapter One

Sacred, Daemonic, Profane

We are all familiar with the word 'religion': we use it freely, with reference to what is at least an observable component within practically all human existence. But it is a somewhat more complex word than it looks. Even its etymology is uncertain.

What *is* religion?

There are some of us who understand it primarily, or even totally, in terms of *being good*—perhaps in some particular way or with some particular motivation or in some particular mood. Thus Matthew Arnold could assure us that "The true meaning of religion is . . . not simply morality, but morality touched by emotion":[1] thus we sometimes find the act of going to church interpreted as a claim of superior virtue, which is rather as though the act of going to the hospital were to be interpreted as a proud boast of exceptional health. Christianity is then seen primarily as an ethical system and Jesus as an ethical teacher—often with the very un-historical implication that "Love your neighbour as yourself" was an original idea of his own and the distinguishing mark of his followers. On this reckoning, no distinction between religion and morality would be possible.

[1] Matthew Arnold, *Literature and Dogma*, I.2.

17

The trouble is that this view of the matter hardly fits the observable facts, unless we do violence to the common-usage sense of that word 'religion'. There are many people who have high moral standards and who live up to them punctiliously, while firmly and even fiercely claiming to have no 'religion' at all. In certain cases we may be able to say that they are deceiving themselves and are in fact deeply 'religious', although at some unconscious level. But if we said this dogmatically and about every such case, we would be going beyond any possible evidence and on arbitrary lines.

Contrariwise, it is an old observation that the effect of deeply-felt 'religion' upon conduct can sometimes be very un-ethical or immoral indeed. This is not only a matter of people failing to live up to their own religious ideals and so acting wickedly: it can also be a matter of people acting wickedly in the real or supposed fulfilment of those ideals. Catholics are used to hearing wisecracks about the Inquisition, an institution and policy which I do not propose to defend. But it isn't only us. It was no kind of Christianity that Lucretius had in mind when he commented with horror upon the evils to which men can be driven by religion;[2] and many later writers have argued that in moral and ethical terms and so far as human well-being is concerned, 'religion' has done much more harm than good.

I do not propose to consider that question here, but only to observe that religion and morality are distinct subjects. There is plainly a close relationship between them, and an extremely close relationship in Christianity. It can be argued (though some would disagree

[2] Lucretius, *De Rerum Natura*, I.101.

violently) that every moral judgment must presuppose some antecedent view of life and the human condition, essentially religious in nature if not consciously and explicitly so: it is clearly true that every religion will have its implications for conduct. But the distinction remains. Somebody once observed that while men tend to be moral but irreligious, women tend to be religious but immoral. One might dissent from so sweeping and sexist an observation, while conceding that the distinction so drawn is a real one.

Religion is not *simply* a matter of being good, and least of all when the 'goodness' in question is conceived in horizontal and humanitarian terms alone.

Many of us, recognising that it includes a vertical component as well or primarily, would explain its core-meaning in terms of God. There are those who believe in God and those who do not. Anyone who does believe in him, and whose life is affected by that belief in some measure, can be described as having a religion, whereas the atheist has none. God can of course be given a number of different names—Yahweh, Allah, and so forth—and can be conceived as standing in various relationships, of immanence or transcendence or both, to the visible world of our experience: further beliefs about him can vary substantially, and it is most misleading to say—as people often do—that the world's great religions differ in externals but are centrally one. The converse generalisation would come closer to the mark.

But however religions may differ, it is felt, they are all built around the concept of a Supreme Being; and if we are to embark upon a serious enquiry of the religious kind, the first thing we shall need to know is whether such a Being exists or not. "Is there a God?" asks St. Thomas at the beginning of the *Summa* (and he goes on to say "Apparently not"): this may well strike us as an entirely logical manner of proceeding. We cannot embark upon any further theology until we know whether there's a *Theos* for it to be about.

I do not in the least wish to play down the importance of that primary question—its importance, that is, for actual belief and therefore for conduct. If the atheists are right, if there is no God, all further belief will only be of interest to those who specialise in the psychopathology of delusion, which is very much how Freud saw the matter. But if there is a God, it will be the atheists who are living in a dream-world, out of touch with reality. So we must ask the first question first.

But it cannot retain its primacy if we want to consider 'religion' from the outside, broadly and in comparative terms. We shall then find certain outlooks and systems which will have to be called 'religious', but in which the concept of a Supreme Being—as understood by ourselves—plays only a limited and ambiguous part. It will hardly be denied that Hinduism and Buddhism are both 'religions', of great subtlety and importance as such. Yet if we ask whether a Hindu or a Buddhist believes in God, the answer has to be equivocal, at least so far as our understanding of the words 'believe' and 'God' is concerned. Then there are any number of cults and faiths which include some more or less clear-cut notion of a Supreme Being and even a Creator, but which put all the emphasis elsewhere. God exists, but he is only invoked (if at all) at times of exceptional crisis and despair: he is not central to the people's religion as normally lived from day to day.

The student of comparative religion therefore finds some difficulty in defining his subject-matter. If the concepts of 'morality' and 'God' are insufficient for this purpose, separately or taken together, what further and perhaps more basic concept does he need? There has to be something: otherwise we would be driven to the absurd conclusion that the word 'religion' has no meaning at all.

It has been widely found that the best working answer to that question is one that makes 'sacredness' into the most basic concept. For the purposes of this book, therefore, I go along with those numerous specialists who accept Durkheim's lapidary statement of the case: "The division of the world into two domains, the one containing all that is sacred, the other all that is profane, is the distinctive trait of religious thought."[3]

Some believers will object to that definition, claiming to see all reality as 'sacred' and nothing at all as 'profane': some will see a pagan and pre-Christian falsity in that whole dichotomy, and indeed in the whole idea of 'religion' as something separate and special.

Their objections will come up for consideration in a later chapter. My present purpose is purely descriptive: here, I am not concerned with any actual rights and wrongs, but only with the question of how most people have seen things. In that preliminary sense, there is undoubtedly a field of enquiry and consideration that can be called 'religion'; and we can most usefully define this

[3] Emile Durkheim, *The Elementary Forms of the Religious Life* (London: George Allen and Unwin, 1971), 37. Here as elsewhere, the details given are those of the edition actually cited: they are not repeated subsequently, and the pagination of other editions may differ.

as the field or area within which people apprehend this or that as 'sacred' and respond to it accordingly.

Even the most superficial study of anthropology and comparative religion will make it clear that for most peoples at most times, certain objects and places and individuals and activities and phenomena have been 'sacred' while others have been more or less totally 'profane'. There can be grey areas and marginal cases, but the distinction is usually clear enough.

The nature of this dichotomy deserves attention. It looks straightforward enough: if we heard it said that something was or was not 'sacred', most of us would have at least some idea of what the speaker meant. But if we tried to define his meaning with any precision, we would run into some curious difficulties. 'Sacredness' would turn out to be a very elusive quality. "At bottom, the only helpful thing one can say of the sacred in general is contained in the very definition of the term: that it is the opposite of profane. As soon as one attempts to give a clear statement of the nature, the *modality* of that opposition, one strikes difficulty."[4] One can of course vary the angle by using the various near-synonyms of 'sacred': one can speak of the 'holy' or the 'numinous'. But the difficulty will still remain: everything of that kind "completely eludes apprehension in terms of concepts. The same thing is true (to take a quite different region of experience) of the category of the beautiful."[5] The 'sacred' or 'holy' or 'numinous' "is perfectly *sui generis* and irreducible to any other; and therefore, like

[4] Roger Caillois, as quoted in *Patterns in Comparative Religion* by Mircea Eliade (New York: Sheed and Ward, 1958), xii.

[5] Rudolf Otto, *The Idea of the Holy* (Oxford: O.U.P., 1958), 5.

every primary and elementary datum, while it admits of being discussed, it cannot be strictly defined."[6]

Nor will the words themselves give us much help. 'Profane' seems clear enough: it refers to whatever we find in front of the temple (*pro fanum*) and therefore outside it, to whatever lacks the religious kind of importance. The 'sacred' will then be whatever *does* have the religious kind of importance. But any such definition of it will be circular: as we have seen, any fruitful use of words like 'religion' and 'religious' will imply some prior concept of the 'sacred', and cannot therefore define that concept.

Nor will the origins of 'holy' help us much. That word is related to 'health' and also to 'whole': its root appears to have signified either 'of good augury' or 'inviolate'. Such meanings are positive enough but seem to miss the point: to modern ears, the note they strike suggests the profane rather than the sacred. The developed sense of the word is clearly religious. But in popular usage at least, it has been narrowed down to mean only a certain quality—of virtue and spirituality— in the life of a human individual. In this sense, it would mean nothing to attribute 'holiness' to (say) a physical object or a biological process. Catholics have traditionally made use of 'holy water': I, at least, am conscious of a certain semantic unease when thus speaking of it. It does not differ from other water precisely as a saint differs from other men.

So 'sacred' itself needs to be put under the microscope. In their common origin (the verb *sancire*), the Latin words *sacer* and *sanctus* involve the idea of something

[6] Ibid., 7.

marked off and made separate and inviolable under penalty, which comes close to the idea of *taboo* or ritual prohibition. So, in the developed sense of the word, "Sacred things are those which the interdictions protect and isolate: profane things, those to which these interdictions are applied and which remain at a distance from the first."[7] This is a useful line of analysis, but it only offers us a means of *identifying* the sacred: it is that to which certain cautions, prohibitions, or interdictions are deemed appropriate. Its distinctive quality, prompting such responses, remains undefined and perhaps undefinable. It may prove to be a fact of primary experience, not capable of being defined in terms of anything more basic.

There is therefore a certain *prima facie* case for arguing, as some do, that 'sacredness' is a wholly unreal or fictitious quality. The trouble is that the same would then need to be said of such similarly irreducible qualities as 'goodness', 'beauty', and 'truth'; and this would take us onto philosophically shaky ground, as well as involving us in an undemocratic and barbarian rejection of practically all human experience.

'Sacredness' may indeed be undefinable, but is not necessarily unreal on that account. For most people, in fact, "the sacred is pre-eminently the *real*. . . . Religious man's desire to live *in the sacred* is in fact equivalent to his desire to take up his abode in objective reality, not to let himself be paralyzed by the never-ceasing relativity of purely subjective experience, to live in a real and effective world, and not in an illusion."[8]

[7] Durkheim, *Religious Life*, 40–41.

[8] Mircea Eliade, *The Sacred and the Profane* (New York: Harper and Row, 1961) 28.

It might reasonably be asked, at this point, why so seemingly positive a concept as 'sacredness' should ever have been associated with taboos, prohibitions, cautions, interdictions, and similarly negative responses. If the sacred is the supremely real, should we not embrace it without reserve?

In order to ask such a question, one would need to overlook certain polarities which have lurked within that concept from the start; and modern usage makes it easy for us to do so. There are of course certain facetious uses of the word 'sacred'. But when used seriously today, by religious people or others, it is nearly always given an unequivocally positive sense. The sacred is simply the *good*, in however undefinable a mode: the supremely Sacred, God, is the supremely good.

But this simplicity in the word's meaning is a recent development, and a semantic weakening. It was originally a double-edged kind of word. It referred to the quasi-divine, but also—ambiguously—to the quasi-daemonic: it carried overtones of the possibly dangerous, the possibly defiled and evil. "This ambivalence of the sacred is not only in the psychological order (in that it attracts or repels) but also in the order of values; the sacred is at once 'sacred' and 'defiled'. Commenting on Virgil's phrase *auri sacra fames*, Servius remarks quite rightly that *sacer* can mean at the same time accursed and holy. Eustathius notes the same double meaning with *hagios*, which can express at once the notion 'pure' and the notion 'polluted'. And we find this same ambivalence of the sacred appearing in the early Semitic world and among the Egyptians."[9]

[9] Eliade, *Comparative Religion*, 14–15.

This ambivalence has sometimes been seen as a simple confusion of the mind, as when Frazer (echoing Robertson Smith) spoke of the Syrians' attitude to pigs. "Some said it was because pigs were unclean; others said that it was because pigs were sacred. This . . . points to a hazy state of religious thought in which the idea of sanctity and uncleanness are [sic] not yet sharply distinguished, both being blent in a sort of vaporous solution to which we give the name taboo."[10] But while the early Syrians doubtlessly drew certain distinctions in a very imperfect manner, they will hardly have bracketed such seemingly total opposites in mere haziness of thought. They were more probably enacting their own version of a universally-recognised polarity.

Rudolf Otto encountered this when he tried to analyse the idea of the Holy. He found it necessary to speak here of a *mysterium tremendum et fascinans*,[11] and all three words deserve attention. The 'holy' or 'sacred' is above all mysterious. We cannot understand it, we cannot pin it down in words: we might even say that anything fully named, fully defined, is 'profane' by that token alone. The 'sacred' also fascinates us: it holds our attention, we are drawn to it most powerfully. But it fills us with a kind of terror as well and so repels us: one part of our split minds would wish to escape from it altogether and have nothing whatever to do with it.

This polarity was present from the start in the Judaeo-Christian tradition, although somewhat obscured by certain present-day theologies. The *tremendum* side of God became his 'wrath' in the Old Testament, and per-

[10] J. G. Frazer, "Spirits of the Corn and the Wild", *The Golden Bough*, Pt. 5 (London: Macmillan, 1914), II, 23.

[11] Otto, *Idea of the Holy*, 12 and *passim*.

haps by something more than a mere anthropomorphic analogy:[12] the *fear* of the Lord was the beginning of wisdom though not its end, and when the Christian addresses God as his Father, he needs to remember that fatherhood was a much more authoritative and alarming affair in New Testament times than it is today. Nor did Incarnation eliminate this element of the *tremendum*. One kind of easy piety addressed itself, as though cosily, to "Gentle Jesus, meek and mild": some would now domesticate him on different lines, making him the "man for others" above all, the supremely unselfish and socially good guy. But the Creeds, not to mention his own words, speak of Jesus also as the dreaded Judge who may one day fling you and me out of his sight. So even here, the Divine can turn out to be—from our point of view, and by our own choice—the Satanic, in the sense of proving the ultimate Adversary.

Such polarities, too easily forgotten nowadays, need to be borne in mind in any further consideration of the 'sacred'. If we cannot define this, we can identify it easily enough by people's responses to it; and within these, there will usually be a powerful ambiguity. They desire simultaneously to embrace and to avoid it.

The power of such feelings is noteworthy in itself: they seem quite disproportionate by any functional or profane standard. We often experience strong emotions, positive or negative, for clearly sufficient reasons, as when one receives a large and unexpected cheque or a diagnosis of terminal cancer. The emotions aroused either way by the sacred have no such obvious justification. Those who do not share them, having some

---

[12] See ibid., 18: some would disagree.

different notion of the sacred or perhaps none at all, may be disposed to interpret them in pathological terms.

They always include that note of fear, the sacred being *tremendum* as well as *fascinans*. But this is not, or not simply, the kind of fear that is aroused by simple danger. C. S. Lewis makes the distinction well. "Suppose you were told there was a tiger in the next room: you would know that you were in danger and would probably feel fear. But if you were told 'There is a ghost in the next room', and believed it, you would feel, indeed, what is often called fear, but of a different kind. It would not be based upon the knowledge of danger, for no one is primarily afraid of what a ghost may do to him, but of the mere fact that it is a ghost. It is 'uncanny' rather than dangerous, and the special kind of fear it excites may be called Dread."[13] 'Awe' might be a better word, since 'dread' has become somewhat devalued: one can 'dread' an examination, a bank statement, even a tedious party. One's feelings about the ghost, if one believes in it, are of a different kind.

Auden states the matter in terms of the imagination. "Some sacred beings seem to be sacred to all imaginations at all times. The Moon, for example, Fire, Snakes and those four important beings which can only be defined in terms of nonbeing: Darkness, Silence, Nothing, Death."[14] Some of these 'beings' can of course be feared not as the ghost is but practically as the tiger is, in terms of simple danger: we have ample cause to be afraid of Death and often of Fire and Snakes, and even

[13] C. S. Lewis, *The Problem of Pain* (London: Geoffrey Bles, 1940), 8.

[14] W. H. Auden, *The Dyer's Hand* (London: Faber and Faber, 1963), 55–56.

sometimes of Darkness, within which enemies may lurk. The awe aroused by these things may well have certain psychological roots in simple fear of the most practical and prudential kind. But this is clearly not true of the Moon, which has never been able to do us any mischief at that level, but which has none the less been almost universally seen as sacred,[15] and is still so seen by our instinctive selves. When men first landed on its surface, the most hard-boiled and materialistic of us must have found it hard to fight down a superstitious fancy that mankind was there guilty of a collective profanation or sacrilege.

The sacred always evokes feelings of awe, but these are not to be fully explained away in terms of simple and physical fear that has run to seed in ignorant minds. The two things are closely but not simply related.

I have never seen a hydrogen bomb. Crudely and in ignorance, I imagine it as a substantial metal cylinder, carrying various stencilled instructions and warnings and having various controls recessed into its surface. However that may be, it is a device—commonly so called by journalists—and as such, it lies wholly within the profane realm of technology. Yet if allowed to gaze upon such a device, I am quite sure that I would experience feelings of awe. These would be practically unrelated to any possible apprehension of immediate danger. I would assume that the safety-precautions of those who managed the thing approached perfection: it would be most unlikely to go off in my presence, and even if it did, it could do nothing worse to me than might be done by a skidding car or a lunatic's gun. I

---

[15] Eliade, *Comparative Religion*, ch. 4.

would hardly be in physical fear at all, over and above our common fear of nuclear war. But I would feel that I was confronting what Eliade would call a kratophany, a symbolic manifestation of power—and of a destructive power so immense that the imagination can only apprehend it as total. To me, it would be an ikon of Hell, and in that sense—the negative or daemonic sense—a sacred object. I could not possibly see it as just another piece of ironmongery, or even (moralistically) as just another instance of government villainy, though it would be both in fact.

Any apprehension of sacredness, in either of its two contrasted senses, has an effect of changing the subject. It overshadows all questions of mere technology, of how we are to do this or that and so achieve desired results: more surprisingly, perhaps, it can also overshadow all questions of mere social morality. Sacredness is an irreducible absolute: it demands a total response, neither simply prudential nor simply ethical in nature.

We can identify the sacred in terms of how people feel about it, but also in terms of what they do about it. They handle it very carefully indeed and according to set rules and precedents: never casually, never permissively, very often ritually.

Profane things also may need very careful and controlled handling. The technicians involved with that hydrogen bomb may attribute no sacred quality to it, but they will undoubtedly be subject to strict regulations. Many technologies and materials involve danger, and so need to be treated with what will commonly —and significantly—be called 'respect'. The consequent behaviour-patterns will be laid down in some book of rules and enforced by some authority: if they were witnessed by some outside observer who knew nothing of the dangers involved—a social anthropologist from Mars, let us say, green and web-footed—he would probably take them to be purely ritual or ceremonial in nature, and he might speak loftily of superstition or neurosis. (He might make a similar mistake about surgery. The robed and masked High Priest, the attendant Virgins, the ritual ablutions, the prostrate victim, the infinitely careful observance of a hundred rubrics —would not all this add up, clearly enough, to the ancient rite of human sacrifice, a variant of what the Aztecs used to do?)

The distinction between functional and ritual behaviour is not always as absolute as it looks to us. Practices that now seem wholly ceremonial may well have seemed wholly functional in earlier times, especially where sacredness was believed to pervade all things, so making 'religion' into the basis of all life instead of a separate and specialised activity. "Originally, all behaviour, all knowledge, all relationships, all institutions, were rooted in concepts of the supernatural. Early farming was organised in terms of carrying out routines, often highly ritualised, which had been laid down by tradition, with divine sanctions as their guards. Building was similarly controlled by sanctified routines. Early medicine was concerned to manipulate supernatural forces, and illness itself was commonly thought to be evidence of divine wrath."[16] Such a mental 'set' would tend towards the elimination of the profane: only the wholly trivial would

[16] James Hemming, *Individual Morality* (London: Nelson, 1969), 52.

lack religious importance. It would also make for an extreme conservatism. All things must be done in the time-honoured way and with the full ritual of our ancestors, and for reasons which are indistinguishably pious and prudential. It will be a shocking thing in itself if we offend the gods by ritual carelessness or impurity, but it will also cause the harvest to fail and our wives to be barren and our children to die.

People can thus respond to the sacred as to a threatening *tremendum*; and it is probably true that all notions of sacredness have certain psychological roots in straightforward fear of possible disaster and in a consequent adherence to well-tried patterns of behaviour.

But this can hardly be the whole story. It explains fear but not awe. The sacred can then be seen as *tremendum* and as holding out attention on that account, but it can hardly be seen as *fascinans* in any further sense: God or the gods may well be seen as dangerous Powers whom we need to placate for our own good, but hardly in terms of the supremely and wholly Desirable. "It may well be possible, it is even probable, that in the first stage of its development the religious consciousness started with only one of [the poles of the 'sacred']—the 'daunting' aspect of the numen—and so at first took shape only as daemonic dread. But if this did not point to something beyond itself, if it were not but one 'moment' of a completer experience, pressing up gradually into consciousness, then no transition would be possible to the feelings of positive self-surrender to the numen."[17] Without such a transition, religion would be hardly

[17] Otto, *Idea of the Holy*, 32.

more than a method, even a technology, for coping with certain kinds of danger.

It can always sink to that level. Even Christians, of the more nominal and self-regarding sort, can come to see their Faith and all its requirements as a kind of insurance-policy against the flames of Hell.

But it then ceases to be a religion, a real apprehension of the sacred under both its aspects—a certain fear of the Lord, yes, but the love of God as well. A better Christian serves God in worship and virtue for God's sake alone, or primarily at least. He will not altogether transcend the ambivalence of the sacred. The danger of his own damnation—of eventually meeting a God who turns out to be, for him and by his own choice, the Adversary or Enemy and in that sense Satanic—may not bulk very large in his day-to-day consciousness and devotion. But like St. Paul, he will bear it in mind to some degree, avoiding the dangerous mistake of the Quietists: his behaviour still needs to be careful.

So, at the higher levels of pre-Christian religion, the gods come to be seen as deserving our respect and service, in themselves and not only because of what they may do to us if offended. *Pietas*, felt in the heart and acted out in behaviour, becomes a natural instinct as well as a duty and precaution.

There are therefore two levels, of prudence and of piety—corresponding to the two adjectives *tremendum* and *fascinans*—at which careful and controlled behaviour is mankind's universal response to anything apprehended as sacred, as a presence and operation of the great *mysterium*. The consequent codes of ritual and prohibition and taboo vary immensely as between different cults and cultures, but they are always taken very seriously by the people involved. Where they come to seem irrelevant or pointless, this invariably shows that the thing in question has ceased to be seen as sacred.

The behaviour-controls of religion, of *pietas*, are seldom limited to morality and worship. Some of them may well be linguistic. We respond to the sacred in our speech, and notably in that highly-charged and ritual kind of speech called poetry: within limits, we can identify the sacred by the poets' concentration upon it. But it also calls for a special kind of language in daily life. This will usually be reverential, calling perhaps for lowered voices and for a manner which, when seen from the outside, may seem stilted and artificial. There may well be euphemisms and circumlocutions: any brutal frankness of speech may seem disrespectful in the extreme, and it may only be deemed proper for the sacred to be mentioned by certain people or on certain special occasions, and perhaps in a special idiom or even in a separate language that will probably be an archaic one.

A superficial observer might misunderstand all this. From the carefully distanced manner in which people naturally talk about the sacred, he might infer that they took it to be something simply nasty.

His mistake would be real but not total. Ambivalences run all through the field of 'religion' as most broadly conceived. If the sacred is recognised by that careful and distanced kind of speech, it can also be recognised by a studied irreverence, a counter-ritual of disrespect or abusiveness which (when seen from the outside) seems as disproportionate as its converse. The anti-clerical joke flourishes where Catholic faith is strongest, real blasphemy would be impossible in a fully atheistic society. Even a religious office or function can be a very double-edged thing. In many primitive cults, the man marked out for sacrifice is deemed to be a sacred being. He is then regarded as wholly innocent *and* wholly guilty, and is treated accordingly: he is given honours and pleasures and privileges, *and* he is subjected to the ultimate in ritual degradation and violence. The only option ruled out is any common or casual treatment of him, just like that given to ordinary people.

In so far as sacredness can be defined at all, it can be defined in those terms. The sacred is *that which needs to be approached and handled in a special way*—a way to which all practical and functional considerations are simply irrelevant, and which must always seem arbitrary and absurd to those who do not apprehend the sacredness in question.

As to what constitutes the sacred and therefore needs that kind of controlled and ritual treatment, people's ideas have varied enormously. We, inheriting the Judaeo-Christian tradition as our mental background at least, see it most naturally in terms of that exceptionally spiritual tradition—perhaps only in terms of a wholly transcendent God, perhaps (if we are more incarnational by training or instinct) in terms of his immanence as well, and therefore of various explicitly sacred buildings and rites and individuals and objects and so forth. We may be surprised, and possibly even shocked, when we see how widely the net is cast by others. We may suspect them of that idolatry which our tradition has always regarded as supremely evil.

We may then do them an injustice. The Judaeo-Christian tradition is not unique in saying that there is one God, the unseen Creator and Sustainer of all things: it is only unique, or at least highly distinctive, in placing him at the centre of religious life and in limiting the number of hierophanies, of his genuine manifestations. Some kind of belief in such a God—the ultimately sacred, the ultimate and unfathomable One—is found within practically all religions everywhere, no matter how polytheistic and idolatrous they may seem to us. But as I have observed, he is often kept in the background. Religious thought and activity is primarily centred around things seen as manifestations of him or of some lesser sacredness; and these are seldom 'worshipped' in the fully idolatrous sense of being identified with God himself. (A Catholicism in decline can sometimes display the same tendency. The One God is by no means denied. But something else lies at the emotional heart of things— some local saint or cult, perhaps, or some real or alleged apparition, together with certain public preoccupations of the moment. I have met Catholics of the fiercest orthodoxy, whose deepest feelings were none the less reserved for three things not mentioned in their Creeds or their liturgy—Communism, abortion, and Fatima.)

Outside this Judaeo-Christian tradition, almost anything can be seen as sacred, as manifesting the Divine in some outstanding fashion. "We must get used to the idea of recognizing hierophanies absolutely everywhere, in every area of psychological, economic, spiritual and social life. Indeed, we cannot be sure that there is *anything* —object, movement, psychological function, being or even game—that has not at some time in human history been somewhere transformed into a hierophany."[18] This

[18] Eliade, *Comparative Religion*, 11.

fact creates danger for the traveller, even today. He can give unintentional offence. When visiting a Christian church, the well-mannered unbeliever will not spit on the floor. But any one of us, when a guest in some country and culture very unlike his own, can offend in just that way by some action which seemed to him to have no religious implications at all.

It might therefore be argued that nothing can actually *be* sacred—that 'sacredness' is a wholly subjective and even fictitious quality, projected upon this or that by social convention of a logically random kind, not actually residing in anything at all. Many people would see this as an obvious and total truth.

I shall return to this question later. For the moment, I shall only point out that such reductionist arguments would carry more weight if the attribution of sacredness were wholly random. In fact, it is not. As Eliade observes, almost anything *can be* seen as a hierophany, as sacred. But there is a large area of practical consensus: we can draw up a short and coherent list of things that almost universally *are* seen as sacred by primitive or pre-scientific man—the sky, the Sun, the Moon; water, stones, trees; the earth and its vegetable fertility, woman and her human fertility; certain focal points in time and space.

But it would be rash, in my opinion, to make too much of any such consensus. A kind of romantic primitivism might perhaps dispose us to see it as a collective perception of the real, an objectively valid though pre-scientific wisdom. Perhaps it is; but (I would say) only in the secondary and wholly subjective sense of a poetic apprehension that has been shared by many. Those who study the poet's art will often find it most useful and illuminating to distinguish the 'sacred' from the 'profane'.[19] But their use of both words will then differ subtly and crucially from the sense they have for the student of comparative religion and for the theologian.

We should certainly pause before dismissing that consensus as a collective delusion, a recurring pattern of the folly that stems from fear and ignorance. But if there is any possibility of a genuine and objective sacredness, its apprehension will need some more solid basis than that.

So far, I have been trying to emphasise three observable facts about 'religion', considered as a human phenomenon and in the widest possible sense of the word. In the first place, it is something distinct from morality, however closely the two may be intertwined in practice. Secondly, it needs to be defined in terms of the apprehended 'sacred' as against the 'profane'. And finally, that dichotomy is not simply a matter of the good as against the evil.

Its real nature can be illustrated by an analogy drawn from common experience. This often suggests that the opposite of love is not hatred but indifference. Love and hatred have a great deal in common. They can co-exist in deep ambiguity (*odi et amo*): each can lie concealed behind an outward appearance of the other: each can startle us by its sudden transformation into the other. And while it is usually unpleasant to be hated, there is a certain sense in which it is far more wounding to be regarded with indifference. The person who hates you does at least care: he takes you seriously as an individual, and in this he resembles the person who loves you. For many

[19] See Auden, *Dyer's Hand*, for many instances.

aspects of your emotional life, the big difference will be between these two, taken together, and those others who don't care about you one way or the other.

We can thus speak of love-hate (within limits) as a single thing, amounting to deep emotional involvement, and of indifference as its opposite. But those who are indifferent to you are not wicked people or your personal enemies: you may in fact find that their company has its distinctive attraction, as being restful and undemanding.

So with that other dichotomy, taken so very seriously by most peoples though much less by ourselves. This concerns a specific kind of importance, attributed to this but not to that, and with implications that can be positive or negative or both in complex ambiguity. 'Sacred' is not a simply positive term, nor is 'profane' a simply negative term. The realm of the sacred includes Satan as well as God, curses as well as blessings, the Mass but the Black Mass too: if it normally excludes such things as technology, this does not mean that they are evil or immoral, but only that in themselves, they lack momentousness of the religious kind. This makes them restful and undemanding in their way, like your more detached acquaintances.

It's as in your emotional life: sacred-daemonic corresponds to love-hate there, and profane to indifference. Neither quite corresponds to the difference between the good and the bad.

I suggest that this conceptual framework will help us to resolve certain misunderstandings of the ethical or moral sort. The surface question is "Should we do XYZ or not? Is it right or wrong?" As so posed, it can be the subject of simple disagreement. But beneath it, possibly below the level of consciousness, there may lie the deeper question of "Does XYZ lie within the realm of the sacred? If so, how careful must we be about its daemonic potential? Or does it lie wholly within the realm of the profane?" If questions of this kind are present but unrecognised, the two sides are likely to be at cross-purposes. Their difference may seem to resemble the familiar moral and casuistical difference between those who are more rigorous and those who are more easy-going, but only on the surface. Beneath that, there can be a real if unconscious 'disparity of cult'. The two sides, although formally united under a single cultic or denominational label, may differ radically in their apprehension of the sacred-daemonic as against the profane, and also (perhaps) of the positively sacred as against the daemonic. In a root sense, they will be of different 'religions': it may not be too much to say that they are worshipping different gods.

The subject of this book is, I suggest, a case in point.

Chapter Two

The Goddess of Love

John Milton wrote a long and lofty poem about the Fall of Man; and in the course of it, he saw fit to depart from the words of Genesis—and from most Christian interpretations of these words—in order to tell us, fairly and squarely, that Adam and Eve consummated their love *before* the Fall. At one or two points, therefore, the subject-matter of his narrative had to become sexual.

The passages in question are of course extremely reticent by the standards of present-day fiction, in which we regularly find sexual activity described in every last anatomical and almost acrobatic detail. But there is another respect in which Milton's method here differs sharply from that of most modern novelists. Like a few of these but unlike the great majority, he speaks of sex in the language of religion, telling us how our first parents embarked upon "the Rites Mysterious of connubial Love", and continuing with a kind of hymn in praise of married bliss, this being couched in an idiom that verges upon the ecclesiastical.[1]

To the modern reader, the effect so given may seem strained and unreal. The word "Rites", with its suggestion of high ceremonial, may seem remarkably unsuitable for so very informal an activity; and to make matters

[1] John Milton, *Paradise Lost*, 4. 742–43 et seq.

worse, the word "Mysterious" probably retained some echo of its old and sacramental meaning in Milton's day. In this context, it does not merely remind us that many questions in sexual physiology were then unanswered, or that sexual activity is normally concealed from the prying eyes of others.

We here encounter a sharp dividing-line. In that use of religious language for sexual matters, Milton shows himself to lie on one side of it, together with the vast bulk of common or natural humanity: we, or most of us, lie on the other. I have observed that different pre-modern peoples vary considerably in their notions of what constitutes the sacred. But there is a certain consensus, and there is one point of near-total unanimity. Whatever may be regarded here or there as profane, a momentous sacredness is nearly always attributed to the genital and especially the female functions. Under whatever local name and with whatever practical consequences, Venus or Aphrodite is seen as a goddess. Certain thoughts and words and deeds take us at once into the realm of the sacred, and notably, those thoughts and words and deeds that concern sex.

We shall be theoretically aware of this deep and universal instinct if we have done any reading at all in anthropology, comparative religion, or primitive art. Even then, it will be something that we see and study as from the outside: it is most unlikely to be an inborn mode of our own consciousness, and its full meaning may well elude us. "For non-religious man of the modern societies, [the] simultaneously *cosmic* and *sacred* dimension of conjugal union is difficult to grasp";[2] and

[2] Eliade, *Sacred and Profane*, 146.

while a devout Christian will perhaps claim to know "the experience of a sanctified sexual life" and to deny that this is "no longer accessible in a desacralised society",[3] he may have difficulty in recognising its pre-Christian equivalent elsewhere. An understandable revulsion from the things frequently done in the service of Venus can obscure the genuinely though imperfectly religious nature of that service, so causing it to seem like nothing more than institutionalised wickedness. Something less than justice will then be done to our primitive forefathers.

This is, in fact, an area in which the difference between 'religion' and 'morality' becomes outstandingly conspicuous and important, as does the double-edged quality which 'religion' shares with 'sacredness'. "Religious man sought to imitate, and believed that he was imitating, his gods even when he allowed himself to be led into acts that verged on madness, depravity, and crime."[4] In so far as he did so, we may reasonably judge that his religion needed not only more careful observance but radical reformulation too. I shall be concerned with this necessity later on. But for the present, let understanding come before judgment: let us at least consider the possibility that in attributing sacredness to physical sexuality, primitive or pagan man may have been on to something—a kind of religious wisdom, still active in Milton's mind and in some later writers, but hardly effective at all in the distinctively modern consciousness.

[3] Ibid., 172.
[4] Ibid., 104.

It might be a kind of wisdom that we need; and its historical association with what Christians consider the grossest immorality should not blind us to its essentially religious nature.

The greatness and power of Venus, the sacredness of our physical sexuality, can be seen in various distinct though related ways. At all times, and perhaps especially at our time, the complexity of her full nature tends to be overshadowed by the obvious foreground fact that she offers supreme delights and is undoubtedly fun. But while she was called 'lover of laughter' (*philommeides*), she was also and in the same breath—by a kind of pun— called 'lover of the reproductive organs' (*philommedes*). In some versions of her story, our Western Venus is born from the fertile Cosmic Egg which is one of her universal symbols: in others, from the foam (*aphros*) that was generated from the severed genitals of Ouranos: alternatively again, she is the daughter of Zeus and Dione and therefore—if Dione was an earth-goddess, as seems probable—of the archetypally fruitful marriage between the rain-giving sky and the receptively fertile earth. She is often represented as emerging from the sea, which is a universal symbol of femaleness and mother-hood, or else from a scallop-shell: Botticelli shows her emerging from the sea and standing upon such a shell, the Greek and Latin names for which (*kteis*, *concha*) also signify the female genitals. To speak more historically, her identity and name may stem from the arrival of Mycenaean Greeks in Cyprus around the thirteenth cen-tury B.C. They already had a fertility-goddess of their own, honoured in little statuettes of a widely-found sort: in Cyprus—later to become the proverbial home of

Aphrodite—they encountered the Babylonian, Assyrian, and Phoenician cult of Ishtar or Astarte or Ashtoreth, a goddess of fertility and love and the sea, whose name they modified so as to bring in that suggestion of the foam-born.

The point is that the divinity of Venus—which we echo whenever we speak of 'venerating' anything at all—was of a distinctive kind. From the start, it was primarily about breeding and birth as seen in cosmically sacred terms, and only secondarily about the pleasures of copulation and the more ambiguous pleasures of being in love. Lucretius the atheist had some harsh things to say about those latter pleasures, which can so easily break down into torment and near-madness: he none the less starts his great poem with an impassioned apostrophe to Venus, as to the *Aeneadum genetrix* or Mother of Rome and the power behind all life.

For all human existence, fertility is a clearly momentous thing. Even today, living in highly technologised societies, we depend absolutely upon the continuing fertility of animals and plants and therefore of the land; and it is in human femaleness and fertility that we all have our personal origins and our only hope of familial or tribal or simply human continuance. And where our existence is seen in primarily religious terms, which is how it mostly was seen until recently, fertility will naturally be seen as having momentousness of a supremely religious kind, perhaps with consequences that we might prefer to call 'magical'. The sculptural honouring and safeguarding of fertility, for example, was not confined to those Mycenaean Greeks or to the Mediterranean peoples in general. "Right across the Old World from the Atlantic to Russia statuettes have been found of a shape which suggests a divine fertility, a concern for pregnancy and increase. These naked female statuettes . . . usually emphasise the breasts, the swollen belly, the buttocks, and sometimes the privates. . . . [They] helped to ensure children for the strength of the community and young for the population of wild animals on which the hunting communities lived in the Ice Age."[5] In that sense, such images—the *Venus of Willendorf* is a famous example—will have been partly 'magical' by intention, being designed to achieve highly practical results on something like cause-and-effect lines.

But they were religious too; and there are further and universal responses to fertility and the genital functions that are unequivocally so, as when an ancient Chinese proverb tells us that sexual intercourse is the human counterpart of the cosmic process.[6] "In all primitive societies the emblems and functions of woman retain a cosmological value,"[7] and no less so where a lesser sacredness is believed to pervade all things. "It is the normal tendency of the primitive to transform his physiological acts into rites, thus investing them with spiritual value. When he is eating or making love, he is putting himself on a plane which is not simply that of eating or sexuality. This is true both of initiatory experiences (first-fruits, first sexual act), and also the whole of erotic or nutritional activity. . . . A real religious experience, indistinct in form, results from this effort man makes to

[5] Geoffrey Grigson, *The Goddess of Love* (London: Constable, 1976), 25.

[6] As quoted in Rollo May, *Love and Will* (New York: W. W. Norton and Co., 1969), 37.

[7] Eliade, *Comparative Religion*, 440.

enter the real, the sacred, by way of the most fundamental physiological acts transformed into ceremonies."[8]

This is indeed a habit of the mind into which we
moderns can only enter with difficulty. "For modern
consciousness, a physiological act—eating, sex, and so
on—is in sum only an organic phenomenon, however
much it may still be encumbered by tabus (imposing,
for example, particular rules for 'eating properly' or
forbidding some sexual behaviour disapproved by social
morality). But for the primitive, such an act is never
simply physiological: it is, or can become, a sacrament,
that is, a communion with the sacred."[9]

The possible sacredness of eating lies beyond my
present subject. We may observe in passing, however,
that it is recognised in one way or another by most
religions and by a great many social codes. Even nowadays, there is a big difference between a formal dinner
and a hastily-grabbed sandwich; and this at least echoes
the difference between the sacred and the profane.

The divinity of Venus lies primarily in her embodi-
ment of the roots of life and renewal, of pregnancy and
birth, of fertility, and therefore of the female mystery as
cosmically seen. She is emphatically a female deity,
Earth-Mother rather than Sky-Father: the part played in
her service by the male is real enough and is less of a
recent discovery than has sometimes been suggested.
Malinowski may have misunderstood his Trobriand
Islanders, and there is now increasing scepticism about
those early Mediterranean societies that were matrilinear

[8] Ibid., 32.
[9] Eliade, *Sacred and Profane*, 14.

because fatherhood was unsuspected.[10] The names of
Attis and Adonis and Tammuz should be enough to
remind us that the celebration and safeguarding of fertility, in vegetation-rites especially, was never a solely
feminine affair. But it had that character for the most
part. Even Priapus, with his exaggerated masculinity,
was more of a comic figure than a great god. He had his
divinity, but it concerned the fruitfulness of vines and
trees and vegetables, as is shown in some of his grossest
representations:[11] he was a god of the garden rather than
the bedroom.

It remains true that the service of Venus normally
involves two people of different sexes; and her divinity
has a further aspect or dimension, which can be approached in terms of that fact.

It is a truth universally acknowledged that the act of
copulation is intensely pleasurable, usually if not always,
for one party if not for both. Such language is in fact
most insufficient. This 'pleasure' differs from the others
in kind, not merely in degree. It is reported that the
facial expression of people in orgasm suggests agony
rather than delight: it is as though they transcended
themselves at that moment, ceasing to be the Charles
and Helen or Peter and Jane of daily routine and assum-
ing new identities, archetypal and tremendous. "In us
all the masculinity and femininity of the world, all that
is assailant and responsive, are momentarily focussed.
The man does play the Sky-Father and the woman the

---

[10] For a diehard statement in the contrary sense, see Merlin Stone,
The Paradise Papers (London: Virago, 1976).
[11] See Grigson, *Goddess of Love*, 75–76.

Earth-Mother; he does play Form and she Matter":[12] they become, briefly, eternal gods.

There is an ancient and influential belief that such feelings are not deceptive—that in favourable circumstances, Venus can fulfil the ultimate purpose of all religion by taking us up to the gates of Heaven and through them, into a full unity with the One; and in fact, not in some briefly comforting escape-illusion. Her service can thus take us directly where the ascetics and mystics go by another and harder road, and where it is sometimes claimed that we can be taken by hallucinogenic drugs. So with the Tamil Saivite saints of southern India, to whom the mating of animals suggested "the inseparable unity of all apparent opposites in the transcendental union of Siva and Sakti. This does not mean that the sexual principle was arbitrarily introduced into the divine but that sex itself is seen as holy because it reflects an essential polarity in God which is the source of his creativity and joy."[13]

Sexual love can thus be seen as 'sacramental' in a full though pre-Christian sense. It effects what it symbolises. It symbolises the resolution of opposites, of all differentiation and multiplicity; and in so doing, it effectively resolves our separation from God. It is perhaps in Tantrism that such thought is taken furthest. But its influence is very widespread; and where we find it gaining new favour in our own time, our cynicism should perhaps be less than total. There will undoubtedly be an element there of simple hedonism, affecting a lofty spiritual motivation most hypocritically: there may also be a

[12] C. S. Lewis, *The Four Loves* (London: Geoffrey Bles, 1960), 119.

[13] R. C. Zaehner, *Hinduism* (London: O.U.P., 1962), 174.

somewhat pathetic desire for mysticism on the cheap. But there may be at least some apprehension of a profound religious truth.

But I would call it a dangerous truth at the best, if only because the sense in which Venus offers us a version of the Mystic Way is so radically unlike the primary sense in which she is a fertility-goddess above all.

These two understandings of her sacredness are perhaps capable of being reconciled. Among the Aztecs, for example, "Sex was regarded as something intrinsically holy, for only in this way could new life arise, only in this complete unity in duality was the symbol of the god Ometecuhtli made upon earth. This was of the very nature of divinity, the male and female that were yet one, the creative power sustaining the universe."[14] But to the sacredness of Venus in that mystical mode, her genital function is more commonly seen as an irrelevance at the best, a positive encumbrance or frustration at the worst. Thus in the so-called *Gospel of Salome*, "the union of man and woman in *barren* orgasm becomes the supreme act, the first androgynous being, the divine form";[15] and according to one most powerful version of the tradition, the ultimate mystical heights are to be attained not in normally consummated intercourse but in *coitus reservatus*, with the genital function held firmly and deliberately in check on the male side. This practice has often been valued, of course, as a means of avoiding pregnancy, and its importance for Hindu and especially Tantric thought stems partly from the belief that seminal reten-

[14] C. A. Burland, *The Gods of Mexico* (London: Eyre and Spottiswoode, 1967), 93.

[15] Jean Guitton, *Great Heresies and Church Councils* (London: Harvill, 1965), 134: emphasis added.

tion amounts to a prudent conservation of vital energies. But a positively mystical value has also been attributed, and widely, to what some call *Karezza*, as against the greater carnality of completed intercourse. For some Hindus, it constitutes "the most perfect representation in the samsaric world of the divine transcendence of all opposites":[16] John Humphrey Noyes saw it in deeply religious terms and made it into a cornerstone of 'Bible communism', as practised in his Utopian community at Oneida Creek; a mediaeval heretic declared that in twenty days of it, "I had learned more wisdom in Valladolid than if I had studied for twenty years in Paris": D. H. Lawrence sang its praises in *The Plumed Serpent*.[17]

There is a certain logic in the desire that this mystical Venus should be sterile. Her cult must always imply some version of an ancient and influential belief, to the effect that what Christians call 'creation' was a bad thing, a primal mistake or misfortune. Its multiplicity is what holds us back from the One, being *maya* or illusion at the best, or perhaps the work of some near-Satanic *demiourgos*: either way, it is what we need to discard and transcend as we move towards illumination and perhaps *nirvana*. Our differentiated sexuality thus comes to be seen as a more or less evil thing in itself, and even as a kind of Fall from an originally androgynous condition, as in Plato and on some rather precarious interpretations of Genesis; and any breeding of new life will be a particularly bad thing. It can only enhance the illusion or promote the evil: it can only impede the great spiritual

[16] Zaehner, *Hinduism*, 114: see also pp. 112–13.

[17] See Aldous Huxley, *Adonis and the Alphabet* (London: Chatto and Windus, 1956), 275–85.

task of resolving all differentiation, all plurality in the One.

There is a sharp parting of the ways here: in the last analysis, it concerns the goodness of this visible creation, and the question of whether its multiplicity needs to be redeemed or simply abolished. The more positive view is taken by Christianity and in the primary cult of Venus the Mother: the more negative view is taken by certain Oriental mysticisms and certain Western cults of the Gnostic or Manichaean kind, and also—although for the most part unconsciously—by those who now reach the same practical conclusion on different lines, telling us to make love but not to have babies.

In respect of Venus and not only in respect of Christ, I would say that we are there faced with an orthodoxy as against a heresy. Either way, however, we are still speaking in religious terms: we are still attributing a sacred and indeed sacramental quality to Venus, and in so doing, we are going along with the common judgment of mankind. In whatever sense and degree and with whatever practical consequences, with the emphasis upon fertility here and mystic union there, humanity has mostly recognised that sex lies within the realm of the sacred.

Human responses to sexuality illustrate this fact. Their patterns are complex and various, always including certain elements of straightforwardly social control. But almost invariably, they also include responses of the characteristically religious kind, observable wherever men apprehend something as sacred. These are initially responses of awe, and then of ritual (as distinct from moral) behavior. Venus also is a *mysterium tremendum et fascinans*. She is a 'mystery' in the original sense of being somehow sacramental, not only as lying beyond our full comprehension; she arouses deep awe and sometimes simple fear in various versions; and her fascination is notorious.

There are many manifestations of all this. Some of them concern the specifically female functions of menstruation and childbirth, which threaten nobody (except the parturient mother) and cannot be objects of simple fear, but arouse awe very widely indeed. The girl or woman may be regarded as *anathema*, in the root sense of 'ritually tainted and set apart': she may have to live alone for the time in question, apart from the males especially, and be subject to all manner of further regulations. She may then be seen as having incurred some kind of pollution until ritually purified for the safety of others. We misunderstand the primitive mind if we interpret such customs moralistically, as though it were sinful to menstruate or have a baby: the point is that in such matters, people felt themselves to be on cosmically dangerous ground.[18]

Then there is the question of the visual and verbal treatment given to sex. Such treatment of the sacred is always cautious and controlled. Among the Jews, the real name of God was not to be uttered: there and among the Moslems, no attempt could be made to represent the Divine graphically. In worship, there is a similar tendency to veil the sacred mysteries simply because they are sacred: the Holy of Holies, the iconostasis, the tabernacle and its veil. The same instinct leads to the wide-

[18] For the complex and widespread taboos affecting menstruation and childbirth, see M. Esther Harding, *Woman's Mysteries* (London: Rider and Co., 1971). 56–58.

spread preference for a liturgical tongue that will suggest sacredness by being archaic or obscure or both: Old Church Slavonic, Tudor English, Latin as against the vernacular. We even find it said that the Koran is too holy to be translated at all without falsification.

Parallel considerations have usually governed the visual and verbal treatment of sex. Anthropologically speaking, total nudity is a rare thing in adults. The genitals, except of small children, must normally be given at least some formal or vestigial sort of covering, though this—by an ambivalence or bi-polarity which recurs throughout this field—can also be a kind of adornment, designed to attract attention as well as to conceal. The Elizabethan codpiece has many primitive counterparts, and the supposedly prudish late Victorians dressed their women, for high social occasions, on lines that now seem sexually suggestive and even kinkily so: for them, the bustle seems to have had the curious appeal that steatopygia had for the Bushmen and Hottentots.

Similar restrictions, and with similar ambiguities, have usually governed any representation of sexuality and the nude in art. Except where some sacred or counter-sacred purpose is intended, this needed to be limited and more or less oblique. In the West, this has usually meant that the male nude can be represented in full detail but only in a demobilised condition, while the female nude can be given no pubic hair and certainly no cleft. This is not simply a matter of Christian morals and the chaste imagination. A painting or statue can obey those rules and yet be highly erotic: the suggestive is notoriously more aphrodisiac than the fully explicit. The point is that any infringement of those rules is a breach of the veil that men naturally draw over the sacred.

So with language. In the modern West, or in its English-speaking regions at least, the only words we have for sexual parts and activities are either clinical or else consciously counter-sacred and even hostile and so (in the negative sense) ritual. The sacredness of Venus was tacitly recognised in the consequent verbal taboos, which were extremely powerful until recently; and even now, we cannot really talk about sex in the ordinary relaxed language of common speech, try as we may. Any attempt to do so is palpably self-conscious and false, as was D. H. Lawrence's attempt to reclaim those famous four-letter words—which are not Anglo-Saxon, as is sometimes said, but common Indo-Germanic—for use in contexts of love and *tendresse*. This has been a semantic impossibility for centuries if not for millennia. "They are the vocabulary either of farce or of vituperation; either innocent, or loaded with the very opposite evil to that which prudes suspect—with a gnostic or Swiftian contempt for the body."[19] Their possible innocence might be questioned. But at the best it is the innocence of farce, of mockery: elsewhere—as is shown by the pattern of their use in non-sexual contexts, and also by their popular synonyms—they are words of violence and contempt, heavily loaded with the male's ancient hatred and fear of the female. Their frequent appearance in present-day poetry and fiction, long after their shock-value has been mostly dissipated, testifies to continuing passions in the anti-sexual sense—a subject to which I shall return later.

The sacredness of Venus can be felt as a burden which

[19] C. S. Lewis, *Selected Literary Essays* (Cambridge: 1969), 174.

we inherit and from which we cannot escape, however hard we try. It is constantly asked, with a pathetic lack of realism, why we can't be simple and frank and *natural* about sex. After all, it's only another bodily function and satisfaction, like eating!

There is nothing new about such desperate assertions. "It would be proper to familiarise the sexes to an unreserved discussion of those topics which are generally avoided in conversation from a principle of false delicacy; and . . . it would be right to speak of the organs of generation as freely as we mention our eyes or our hands": that was Mary Wollstonecraft, writing some two hundred years ago,[20] and despite tremendous effort in more recent times, her aspiration has only found the most limited, local, and somewhat pathological kind of fulfilment.

It was always an unrealistic kind of aspiration. As we have seen, even eating has a kind of sacredness, as have eyes and hands for the Christian at least, our entire bodies being temples of the Spirit. Even so, we can be fairly relaxed and straightforward about such functions and parts.

But not about sex: we all discovered, perhaps at about the age of thirteen, that this is totally unlike any other bodily part, function, or satisfaction.

What we then discovered is what common humanity means when it says that Venus is a goddess—great and good, powerfully momentous as well, and even frightening. She is not to be trifled with: *on ne badine pas avec l'amour*.

---

[20] As quoted in Gordon Rattray Taylor, *The Angel Makers* (London: Secker and Warburg, 1973), 7.

Great care was always needed with the sacred. It was always double-edged and dangerous: it attracted you strongly but scared you as well. An element or threat of the daemonic was always present within it.

This polarity within the sacredness of Venus has been apprehended as widely as that sacredness itself. When seen selectively, the Goddess of Love can seem to offer us nothing more alarming than delight, babies, and perhaps some mode of union with the One. But this was never the whole story.

The daemonic Venus has been seen in various ways, and perhaps most notably in terms of violence and death. Sex and death are closely related things: they "have in common the fact that they are the two biological aspects of the *mysterium tremendum*",[21] as is found by humanity both ancient and modern, not only by the psycho-therapist. "Every kind of mythology relates the sex act itself to dying, and every therapist comes to see the relationship ever more clearly through his patients."[22] It was not for nothing that Venus took Mars, god of war, to be her lover. Violence is an extremely sexy thing, and it is not only in the extreme case of rape that sex can be a violent thing, a matter of cruelty and conquest. It always carries that ancient association with violence and killing and death: if the maternal earth is our womb, it is our tomb as well. "The cult of germination has always been associated with the cult of the dead. The Earth Mother engulfs the bones of her children. They are women—the Parcae, the Moirai—who weave the destiny of mankind; but it is they, also, who cut the threads. In most popular

---

[21] May, *Love and Will*, 109.
[22] Ibid., 103.

representations Death is a woman, and it is for women to bewail the dead because death is their work."[23] "In nature the feminine principle, or as naïve man would say the feminine *goddess*, shows itself as a blind force, fecund and cruel, creating, cherishing, and destroying. It is the 'female of the species, more deadly than the male', fierce in its loves as in its hate. This is the feminine principle in its daemonic form. The Chinese call it Yin, the shadowy power of the female . . . symbolised by the tiger gliding stealthily through the grass, waiting to leap upon its prey with claws and fangs, yet looking all the while sleek, gentle, and catlike, making one almost forget its ferocity":[24] *Vénus toute entière à sa proie attachée.*

Such themes echo through all mythology. "If the mysterious power that women possess could generate new life, it followed that it might also be used to harm and destroy. The Mother-goddess, as the supreme expression of the feminine principle, could therefore be worshipped as a war-deity. The 'virgin Anat' of the Bronze-age pantheon of ancient Canaan is portrayed in her epic as a bloody warrior wading thigh-deep in her enemies' blood. Aphrodite, whom the Romans identified with their Venus, was a patroness of war as well as of love, beauty and marriage."[25] A similar duality was attributed to Freya, her Scandinavian counterpart: Hathor, an ancient Egyptian patroness of cosmic attraction and physical love, was a goddess of death as well:[26]

---

[23] Simone de Beauvoir, *The Second Sex* (London: Penguin Books, 1972), 179.

[24] Harding, *Woman's Mysteries*, 34.

[25] John Allegro, *Lost Gods* (London: Michael Joseph, 1977), 145.

[26] Boris de Rachewiltz, *Black Eros* (London: George Allen and Unwin, 1964), 47.

Shakti, the voluptuous and fertile mother-goddess of India, is also and equally the terrible Kali, who wears a necklace of skulls and carries severed heads that drip with blood: the proto-Aphrodite Inanna of the Sumerians seems to have been more fierce and frightening than attractive, and her successor Ishtar or Astarte of the Babylonians and the Assyrians "appears as the Morning Star, waking men to go fighting in wars: a decidedly violent goddess, a wielder of weapons, as well as the goddess of love".[27]

Some people might try to explain all this away by saying that the old myths were probably composed or compiled by men and so gave natural expression to something already mentioned, the male's ancient hatred and fear of the female. But this is the kind of explanation that chases its own tail: it only works by presupposing what it purports to explain, as when people explain the origins of religion in terms of the fear of the dead. A dead man cannot hurt you: you cannot possibly be afraid of him, or in connection with him, unless awe—or some other religious sentiment—is already present in your mind. So with women and the female principle. Pregnancy and childbirth are certainly 'mysterious' in the modern sense, and hardly less so in our own time, despite a vast increase in physiological knowledge: such things arouse deep curiosity of the more or less scientific kind. But the human male is, in general, stronger than the female: his urge to dominate is at least equal to hers: it is a common observation and the subject of much feminist complaint that he usually succeeds in holding his womenfolk down in some more or less

[27] Grigson, *Goddess of Love*, 27.

subordinate position. At no simply physical level do they give him any cause for apprehension: if he has such feelings towards them, these will be the consequence and not the cause of different and deeper feelings which he entertains already.

Fear of the daemonic Venus has doubtlessly encouraged some men to treat women badly. But it cannot have been a response to apprehended danger or the enigmas of reproductive physiology: it can only have been a kind of metaphysical dread, aroused directly by Venus and not only by her operations. Sacredness is enough to chill anyone's spine.

There are further aspects or versions of the daemonic Venus, reminding us yet again that the 'religious' or 'sacred' is not always the simply 'good'. It will not be denied that her worship—alone, or in conjunction with some spouse or lover or son—has been deeply and widely and most influentially 'religious', in the most elemental sense of that word. "The Semites at one time in their history adored the divine couple made up of Ba'al, the god of hurricane and fecundity, and Belit, the goddess of fertility (particularly the fertility of the earth). The Jewish prophets held these cults to be sacrilegious. From their standpoint—the standpoint, that is, of those Semites who had, as a result of the Mosaic reforms, reached a higher, purer and more complete conception of the Deity—such a criticism was perfectly justified. And yet the old Semitic cult of Ba'al and Belit *was* a hierophany: it showed (though in unhealthy and monstrous forms) the religious value of organic life, the elementary forces of blood, sexuality, and fecundity. This revelation maintained its importance, if not for thousands, at least for hundreds of years."[28] 'Revelation' is perhaps an unsuitable word. But if we call the thing in question an 'insight' alone, it remains an insight of the most profoundly and universally religious sort.

But one does not need to be a Christian, or even a Hebrew prophet, to see something positively daemonic—not simply immoral—in some of the practices that follow, reasonably enough, from the premises of any such religion, revelation, or insight.

Sacred prostitution, in one version or another, has often followed from it as though naturally. It shocked Herodotus when he encountered it at Ishtar's Babylonian temple in the fifth century B.C., and we shall not necessarily be primly moralistic if it shocks us as well—and perhaps more so, not less so, when we remember that it was seen at the time in no such adversative light as the word 'prostitution' would now suggest. To the women in question "it was in very truth a *hieros gamos*, a sacred marriage. In it they dedicated their most precious function, namely their reproductive power, to the goddess and avowed that for them spiritual fulfilment, attained through union with the godhead, was more important than biological satisfaction or ordinary human love."[29] In certain cases, ordinary human love was excluded as though deliberately. At her initiation a girl would sacrifice her virginity, nominally to the Great Goddess and possibly to a temple priest in literal fact, but quite as probably to "any stranger who might be passing the night in the temple precincts". In this case, "The rite was performed by two people who had never seen each other

[28] Eliade, *Comparative Religion*, 3–4.
[29] Harding, *Woman's Mysteries*, 137.

before and would in all probability never see each other again. Indeed the regulations prescribed that the stranger should depart before daylight. In this way the non-personal or divine aspect of the rite was impressed upon the participants."[30]

This practice of sacred prostitution, whether initiatory or embraced as a permanent vocation, causes some embarrassment to those who now want us to see the sacredness of Venus in positive terms alone, ignoring her daemonic potential. "Hard though it is for us to conceive how such a custom worked and continued, would this sacramental initiation into the act of love so much have horrified girls brought up to expect it as inevitable and normal? Must we think it worse or more damaging than the legitimized private rape which the beginning of a marriage has so often amounted to, through history? . . . Becoming a temple prostitute up on the rock might have been preferable to slaving in a private house down below."[31] In a way, we can agree: if it comes to that, one born and brought up in a concentration-camp, knowing no other world, might well take the circumstances of life there to be "inevitable and normal". But this fact hardly justifies concentration-camps and the philosophy behind them; and while it is certainly true that some women in every age have preferred prostitution to domesticity and that there can be sexual brutality within marriage, such considerations hardly justify what most of us—for reasons which could as easily be feminist as Christian—would condemn with horror.

It was not only metaphorically that the old Hebrews'

[30] Ibid., 134.
[31] Grigson, *Goddess of Love*, 119–20, 124.

neighbors went *whoring* after strange gods. Some people speak optimistically of 'the brotherhood of all religions', their underlying unity: the eighth chapter of Ezekiel illustrates the insufficiency of all such hopes.

As with sacred prostitution, so with the ritual orgy: the two can shade off into one another. "When the critical moment arrives and the barley starts to germinate, the Ewe negroes of West Africa take measures to ward off disaster by means of ritual orgies. A number of girls are offered as brides to the python god. The marriage is consummated in the temple by the priests, the god's representatives, and the girls, or wives, carry on a sacred prostitution in the enclosure of the sanctuary for some time. This sacred marriage is said to be performed to ensure the fertility of the soil and the animals."[32] Such orgies, generally promiscuous or with some more specific element of individual prostitution, are reported from many quarters—usually with reference to fertility, sometimes with reference to mystic union instead or as well. Here also, the daemonic Venus can cause embarrassment to present-day writers, as to one who finds the highest spiritual wisdom in Tibetan Tantrism and seeks to impart this to the West: he shows a distinct uneasiness when he comes to the sacral orgy, which—since it enables one to transcend one's sexual identity altogether, as union with a single partner does not—plays an important part in that cult.[33]

A recrudescence of such practices—utterly alien to

[32] Eliade, *Comparative Religion*, 354–55, drawing on Frazer: many further instances will be found in de Rachewiltz, *Black Eros.*

[33] See Herbert V. Guenther, *The Tantric View of Life* (Berkeley and London: Shambala Publications Inc., 1972), 97–98.

what we would normally call 'love' as between individuals, whether married or not—is reported from various
quarters in the present-day West. Here, as at some other
points in the 'permissive society', we may reasonably ask
how far hedonism alone is involved and how far an
intended and 'religious' service of the daemonic Venus, a
sexual Satanism.

One aspect of her ancient bloodiness might be deemed
of clear present-day topicality. "It is recorded that . . .
around the sacred stone which represented the goddess
Astarte, hundreds of skeletons of human infants have
been found. She was the goddess of untrammeled love,
and first-born children and animals were sacrificed to
her."[34] It might seem extravagant to say that those small
skeletons have their smaller counterparts in the waste-bins
of countless hospitals and clinics today: the conscious
motivations behind abortion are most unlikely to be
fully 'sacrificial', except perhaps in isolated cases. But we
cannot assume that the service of Astarte had that quality
in any absolute fashion. Although primarily 'religious',
it may also have served as a convenient pretext for
getting rid of the unwanted young; and in any case, if
psychology has taught us anything, it has taught us that
conscious motivations seldom tell all.

If we now find a cult of untrammeled love co-existing
with a large-scale massacre of the innocents, the two
may still be related at some deeper level than that of our
immediate convenience. The blood of our savage ancestors still runs in our veins, and the daemonic Venus is
still as cruel a goddess as ever.

[34] Harding, *Woman's Mysteries*, 138.

Ancient mythology and primitive religion add up to a curiously mixed affair, a big haystack with relatively few needles. "When we speak of myths, as when we speak of ballads, we are usually thinking of the best specimens and forgetting the majority. If we go steadily through all the myths of any people we shall be appalled by much of what we read. Most of them, whatever they may have meant to ancient or savage man, are to us meaningless and shocking; shocking not only by their cruelty and obscenity but by their apparent silliness— almost what seems insanity. Out of this rank and squalid undergrowth the great myths—Orpheus, Demeter and Persephone, the Hesperides, Balder, Ragnarok, or Il- marinen's forging of the Sampo—rise like elms."[35] Something similar can be said of ancient religion, and even of some more recent cults. The Gnostic religion, in its essentials, can be stated very briefly. But the myths in which it found expression are tortuous beyond belief, almost to that point of apparent insanity. At the risk of hurting some people's feelings, I would say much the same about *The Book of Mormon*.

At their best, however, ancient religions and mytho- logies and the associated practices embody a great deal of our race's long experience; and if we receive some fairly unequivocal message from that quarter, we shall do well to take this seriously unless its falsity has since been demonstrated beyond all doubt. It will need translation, of course, into some idiom of our own time, psycho- logical or theological or philosophical or whatever; and while it may then prove to be something that we knew

[35] C. S. Lewis, *An Experiment in Criticism* (Cambridge: C.U.P., 1961), 42.

already, it may possibly prove to be something that we once knew but have since forgotten.

I have suggested three such messages. The first concerns the dichotomy between the sacred and the profane, the second concerns the location of sexuality within the realm of the sacred. But the sexual problem cannot be stated in those positive terms alone. "All healthy men, ancient and modern, Eastern and Western, know that there is a certain fury in sex that we cannot afford to inflame, and that a certain mystery must ever attach to the instinct if it is to continue delicate and sane."[36] So we get a third message: it concerns the fact that in Venus as elsewhere, 'sacredness' is a double-edged and dangerous thing. It includes that "certain fury": rightly do we fear it, as well as feeling ourselves drawn to it most powerfully.

Various objections—philosophical, scientific, and perhaps theological—can be brought against this entire manner of thinking. Let us defer those for the time being and continue to think on these possibly 'primitive' lines.

We shall then face a practical problem. How can we do full justice and piety to the Goddess of Love in all her sacredness, while not laying ourselves open to the terrors and dangers of her daemonic *alter ego*? Can we separate her two selves, embracing the one and rejecting the other? In old myth as in modern experience, they appear to be inter-related past all such separation.

The task is perhaps impossible, unless we find some way of subjecting this great goddess to some kind of transformation, some kind of redemption.

[36] G. K. Chesterton, *The Common Man*, (London: Sheed and Ward, 1950), 125.

Chapter Three

Holy Matrimony

Let us imagine that we are professional students of comparative religion, well grounded in the related subject of anthropology, acutely sensitive to every last nuance of myth and symbol and rite, but tending ourselves towards agnosticism. Let us now suppose that we are given a rare privilege. In some remote corner of a dark continent, hardly affected by the mind of the twentieth century, an archaic and alien folk still observe rituals of immemorial antiquity, not yet documented in the books. We are to visit them, we shall be allowed to witness the most sacred of their rites and earn fame by reporting it to the academic world. Seldom does such an opportunity occur!

So we make the long journey and are kindly received: soon the great moment comes.

The rite in question only takes place once a year; and since it is a rite of renewal and rebirth, it naturally takes place in the spring—at the time when the seeds of corn, having died in the furrow, come thrusting up again to assure the people of daily bread for the coming year. (They have a winter-festival of birth as well, celebrated just after the solstice, as soon as it becomes clear that the sun is not going to die for ever, after all. But we have come too late to see this. which matters little, since its rites are less distinctive.)

Where this spring-festival is concerned, we seem to be on familiar ground: we remember Tammuz and Attis and Osiris, and we have already gathered an impression that the central hero and deity of this alien cult is some kind of corn-god. Nor are we surprised when we learn that the exact date of this ritual is governed by the Moon, which is universally seen as governing all femaleness and therefore all birth. Here, it seems that a special sacredness is attached to one particular vernal reappearance of the New Moon; and her faint light is shining upon us as we enter the midnight temple and join the hushed throng within it.

The rite begins. We crane our necks anxiously, not wanting to miss anything but not wanting to give offence either by any display of profane curiosity. Our professional senses are alert, our notebooks and tape-recorders are inconspicuously at the ready.

What strikes us first when things start happening is that the central part is played, initially, by a *young* man and not by one of the temple elders. We see him walking up slowly between the pillars, under that faint moonlight, holding something stiffly erect in front of him. We look upon this, in its relation to his youth, with professional interest: we have seen such symbols before. It turns out to be a grossly exaggerated candle, just lighted from a newly-kindled and sacred fire, and we now see that everybody present carries a smaller version of it, to which its flame is solemnly communicated. Soon the dark temple is suffused with a flickering multiplicity of candlelight, and only crass insensitivity would fail to respond to the atmosphere of sacredness so created.

The young man advances to the highest and supremely

holy part of the temple, and there he enthrones his tall candle, which may perhaps be wreathed with flowers. Then, to a haunting melody and in an archaic language known to few but the initiates, he sings a long chant in praise and blessing of it.

We are interested but perhaps a shade disappointed. Was our long journey really worth while? Will we have anything so exceptional to report back to our colleagues? All that we have seen so far falls into a pattern that has been familiar to us since student days. Wherever there is to be a springtime celebration of rebirth or resurrection and new life, we naturally expect it to enact the masculine principle with some frankness and emphasis: having seen this done, we know what to expect later on.

We find that we've guessed correctly, though a certain delay is involved. After that enthronement and blessing of the sacred Candle, there are numerous long readings and chantings from the sacred scrolls of these people. In so far as we understand these—we don't know the language very well—we find them broadly poetic and mythological in character, though they are claimed to be of divine origin and to stand in some kind of unique relationship to fact.

But in due course, as we had expected, the rite turns its attention to the female principle. This is represented, predictably enough, by water—the primal womb of all things, Apsu or Tiamat for the Babylonians and Chalchihuitlycue for ancient Mexico, the birthplace of all life (if the scientists are right) and the absolute condition of its survival. We have already gathered that in this present cult, a great though secondary importance is attached to a female figure of the Universal-Mother type, and we note that her name—originally 'Miryam'

—was later modified to mean 'the oceans' (*maria* in Latin), so associating her with this primal element.

The water lies there in a massive stone cup, which we recognise as being a female symbol in itself; and it is one of the temple elders and perhaps the High Priest himself, not that young man, who now approaches it for a long ritual of blessing and celebration.

Finally the great moment comes. He brings the holy and male Candle to the holy and female Water: he holds it aloft: then he plunges it down into the wet depths, working it in and out three times, crying out upon the gods to make this mystical and cosmic marriage a fruitful one. And for final emphasis he pours out his own breath, his *spiritus* or *pneuma* or life, upon the surface of the newly-fertilised water, tracing there a figure of the archetypal *yoni*, the most explicitly female symbol or diagram of all, similar in form to the Greek letter *psi*.

Within the temple, there goes up a faintly audible collective sigh of relief and catharsis. The primal mystery of new life has been re-enacted before our eyes. Calm of mind, all passion spent, the people relax.

The nocturnal rites do not actually end at this point. But what follows, although by no means less sacred, is much less distinctive. It may include the initiation-rites of infants and adults: it will certainly include a solemn re-enactment of the primeval blood-sacrifice around which this entire cult is centred. But these are daily occurrences, whereas the *hieros gamos* or sacred marriage of Candle and Water is a strictly annual event, although faintly echoed a few weeks later. That is the particular distinction of this "truly blessed night", as it is repeatedly called in its chantings.

We are entitled to feel a little disappointment as we

close up our notebooks and prepare to go home. We had hoped to see something really unusual in the way of ritual: instead, we saw nothing that was not already familiar to us in a thousand vegetation-cults and fertility-rites, all round the world and since the dawn of time. As connoisseurs of such things, we may even feel that the symbolism here was altogether too blatant and obvious, even indelicate. The principle of fertility and renewed life can be enacted more subtly than that. We have apparently been among people of somewhat gross mentality.

But we cannot dismiss them out of hand. There is something unique and intriguing about a claim they make at another level. All religions claim to be 'true' in some analogical or poetic sense: these people claim that theirs is 'true' in the literal, factual, or historical sense as well. They talk as though myth and history coincided at a certain point known to themselves—as though cosmic Meaning could somehow take on flesh and blood and had actually done so, walking the streets in human form. We shall need to think this over: unlike the rite that we have just witnessed, it differs crucially from anything that we have met elsewhere in our studies.

The rite has told us a lot, even so. Actions speak louder than words. If we want to know how people really think and feel about something, we must see how they treat it, in daily life and law and routine but above all in deeply-felt ceremony.

The ritual that I have just described is not a product of my own lewd imagination. It is actually and regularly performed like that, in all that explicitness of sexual symbolism, and not only among the depraved and lecherous savages of darkest Bananaland: as the perceptive reader will have surmised, it is in fact the Easter Vigil of the Catholics, their traditional way of celebrating the Resurrection of Christ and the new life that it brings to men. This is the most sacred moment of their liturgical year, celebrated in every one of their churches throughout the world with all the solemnity that circumstances permit. I described it as it might be seen from the outside, by people who knew all about 'religion' in general but little or nothing about Catholic Christianity in particular.

(But I did cheat a little: I described this rite as it was for many centuries, not in the slightly different version that it now takes in most places. The deacon who blesses the Paschal Candle will not always be a young man nowadays: there will not always, or even usually, be that full archaism of chant and language: when the priest breathes upon the water, he will probably do so not in the suggestive shape of the letter *psi* but—more delicately— in the form of the Cross. As for that collective sigh exhaled by the congregation at the climactic moment of cosmic marriage—well, it certainly ought to be exhaled, but I confess that I have never heard it. I suspect that many Catholics keep their attention carefully deflected from the natural symbolism of this rite and concentrated upon its Christian meaning, and would be shocked by any crude insistence upon the former. There are a number of respects in which the Church can be a good deal more shocking than some kinds of Catholic piety would wish it to be.)

In its older version or as now modified, this rite carries a clear message. I do not wish to suggest that it is only—or even primarily—a fertility-rite of the ancient and universal kind, a sexily pagan ritual and no more: to reduce it to that level would be both foolish and offensive. Even so, at a rock-bottom level of symbolism, it does conform itself exactly to that pattern, and thereby offers one major enactment of a principle that is central to my theme.

The Catholic Faith is an incarnational, even a carnal thing: I have heard it described as the sexiest of all the great religions. The uniting of flesh and blood with the supremely Sacred lies at the heart of its belief and its worship too, and a bodily and even sexual emphasis recurs constantly in its self-expression. A Catholic cannot recite his Creeds without mentioning begetting and conception and birth: he cannot say the Hail Mary without mentioning the female generative tract, or the *Te Deum* without praising his Lord for finding there nothing of the indecent or daemonic, nothing to abhor. He sees the whole relationship between God and Man in quasi-sexual or quasi-genital terms: more precisely, he sees human sexuality and the consequent parent-and-child relationship as an ectype or derivative of that archetypal parenthood. He therefore speaks of God the *Father*, knowing perfectly well that no biological maleness is there involved; and when his spiritual writers speak of even a male person's soul in its patient-to-agent relationship to God, they always use a feminine word for it (*anima*) though a masculine word is available (*animus*). His great mystics draw heavily upon erotic and hymeneal imagery when they attempt to speak of the One, the unutterably Pure, as encountered by themselves: finding spirituality throughout the Bible, they find its loftiest intensity in that frankly sensual love-poem, the Song of Songs. Ask a Catholic to name the holiest things that come within his experience: he will list seven hierophanies which he takes to be objective in nature, and *matrimonium* or sexual reproduction will be among them. Even the priesthood receives a degree of sexual definition: the person who sacrifices at the altar must embody, at the derived and human level, the hyper-masculinity of God, and will normally stand in a special and sacrificial relationship to his own sexuality.

The list could be extended. The natural symbolism of that "truly blessed night" does not stand alone and is no kind of anomaly: it is one central element within a larger phenomenon, one that constitutes a prime instance of what I was talking about in the two previous chapters. Towards sex, the primary Catholic response is typical of human response to the sacred.

Such an assertion may seem paradoxical: to some pious ears, it may even seem shocking. Its truth will become obvious, I suggest, as soon as we consider Catholicism as though from the outside and in compara-tive terms, as one religion among others. I am far from believing that it exists among those others on equal terms, with nothing unique in the way of standing and validity: in connection with it, I would therefore say that the comparative method needs very cautious handling. But even here, within limits, that method has its value. Catholic Christianity is not *simply* one religion among many. But it is more than that, not less than that; and there are some purposes for which we can usefully consider it in comparative terms and as 'a religion' in the most basic and universal sense of that word.

As such, it is a shared apprehension of the Sacred and a response to it in action—in the whole of life, but also and notably in action of the controlled and ritual sort, within

which liturgical words and deeds constitute one defini-
tive element. The sacredness thus apprehended is essentially One: it is that of God, and therefore of God-
in-Christ, and therefore of Christ-in-the-Church. But
it has particular hierophanies too, particular manifestations in act; and among these is what the pagan had in
mind when he spoke of 'Venus'. About her, at its primary and ritual level of self-expression, the Church
spoke from the start, and still does speak, in the most
clearly sacral idiom of veneration. She has her place in
the sanctuary, she lies close to the Christian heart of
things. We enacted this fact long before we knew how to
say it: in doctrine as elsewhere, this is the common
pattern of what Newman called 'development'. And we
incurred some rebuke for doing so. In the old days of
sturdy denominational controversy, Protestants sometimes claimed to see in 'Rome' little but a thinly-
Christianised paganism, often with a suggestion that
Venus herself was all too actively present in those gaudy
sanctuaries and in a kind of worship that was considered
'sensual' by the more spiritually-minded and austere.
Such criticisms are still offered, but usually—in our
time—from a more psychological angle: religion is seen
as a sublimation of sexuality, and in those aspects of
Catholicism which I have just been emphasising, a sublimation so glaringly obvious that it shouldn't fool anybody.

The psychological boot may sometimes be on the
other foot. How often, I wonder, is sex used as an
escapist substitute for religion, for God?

But however that may be, the two things are at least
closely related, in Catholicism as elsewhere. It is hardly
enough to say that some part of the Church's message

was always about sex: such words would suggest distinction where we ought to be thinking of unity. But
however artificially, this particular element within the
overall message of love can be separated out and put into
words—words that will not be initially or primarily
moralistic. It will then prove to be a message about
sacredness, and will naturally reflect the double-edged
quality of that concept: in no further sense will it be,
primarily, a message about sin.

We can understand it best, on this reckoning, if we
imagine it as being addressed to the pagan and primitive
mind rather than to people like ourselves. The pagan
already saw Venus as a goddess. Addressing him, the
Church—while correcting that statement of the case—
by no means contradicted its underlying meaning but
took it a good deal further. Its message to him might be
dramatised in the following very un-theological terms:

"Yes, you are right, and more seriously right than you
have ever supposed, or than you probably now desire.
There is no actual being called 'Venus', of course, and
certainly no deity of that name: there is only the One in
Three. But even so, 'the divinity of Venus' will serve as a
good metaphorical way of saying that in this matter of
physical sexuality, we are on holy ground indeed. It is in
fact holier than your natural passions want it to be, and I
am going to make it even more so. From being a mere
hierophany, 'Venus' is now going to become a *sacrament*,
an actual presence and operation of the supremely Holy
and One in his Crucifixion and therefore in his Resurrection, an image also of his fruitful love for myself, his
Bride, and (on your side) an enactment of the union in
God of wholly committed love with generous and therefore vulnerable creativity. That, with no Manichaean

separation of the two, is what your service of her will now mean and be; and in fact, not just in poetic metaphor. Venus is getting a strictly religious promotion from myth into reality: mine is the territory in which myth does become fact, *Logos* or Meaning does become flesh.

"Rightly do you seem alarmed! The sacred potential of Venus will be very much enhanced by this promotion, but so will her daemonic potential; so this particular sacrament will need to be fenced in closely and governed by rubrics as tight as those that will govern my primary and Eucharistic sacrament.

"In addition to all this, there will be very exacting requirements in respect of what I call 'the love of one's neighbour', which includes one's general duty to society. Sex is an area in which one can do immense good or immense harm to others, individually and collectively, and in which new and exacting standards will therefore be put before you: never take them lightly.

"But I'm talking primarily about your treatment of something sacred, forming part of what I call 'the love of God', into whom your supposed 'Venus' has now been subsumed. My cautionary language here will hardly surprise you, in view of your long familiarity with the sacred and its dangers and its exacting requirements; and while the proper service of this transformed Venus will not come easily to you, it will be made possible. The Dying God, the Mortal-Immortal of whom your old mythologies could only dream—he will be with you in person, holding your hand; and if at times he seems to be holding it rather tightly,[1] you may be sure that he knows

---

[1] I have stolen this admirable conceit from Simone Weil.

what he's doing. He knows what it feels like to be a man, he has trodden the winepress alone, he has conquered the world; and his creature Venus, once rebellious, is now among his allies and friends and helpers in so far as she can be seen as being distinct from him at all. So keep her that way! Never forget her newly-enhanced sacredness!"

Any pagan or primitive would get the message, and would recognise its alarmingly positive nature.

With one qualification, I take that to be a fair summary and dramatisation of the Church's message about physical sexuality.

I have perhaps laid too much emphasis there upon the technically sacramental nature of *matrimonium*, which is—in Newman's sense—a fairly recent development. The centrally doctrinal basis of that summary lies elsewhere and is both ancient and simple. There was never any question of sex, or anything else in God's creation, being 'evil' in some inherent or ontological sense; nor was there any question of its being 'profane' and of no specifically religious importance. The Church saw from the start that sex lay within its field and was thus 'sacred', and it spoke accordingly on lines that are often misunderstood nowadays—though not by those who have grasped the central point.

What gets misunderstood is the Church's traditional emphasis—in matters of sexual morality—upon physical actions and formally-defined relationships. From the start, sexual sin was chiefly seen in terms of what you did and who you did it with. There were further sins of thought and willed desire; but these concerned thoughts about physical actions and willed desires to perform them. 'Fornication' and 'adultery' were defined in terms of whether the couple were man and wife or not: 'incest', in terms of their family relationship; 'contraception', 'masturbation', and the 'perversions', in terms of what was done at the physical or bodily level. That's where the moral emphasis always lay; and to some, it seems a grossly sub-Christian kind of emphasis. Doesn't it suggest a preference for law as against love, for letter as against spirit? Isn't it precisely the kind of thing which the Lord rebuked when he found it in the Pharisees? Under the Christian dispensation, are not all such legalisms superseded by the one law of love? About some possible line of sexual behaviour, shouldn't our *only* question concern its tendency to express and promote love or perhaps to hold it back, to frustrate it, to dry it up?

On this reckoning, we would have to conclude that practically all Christians have been radically un-Christian about sex, from the start and with only a few recent exceptions—a conclusion that some bold writers are prepared to accept.

I suggest that they are missing the point. As soon as we start to think comparatively, it ought to become clear that the thing being talked about was not cold law but sacredness, in all the double-edged quality of that concept and with a crucial involvement of the first Great Commandment, not only of the second.

That, primarily, is how I justify the somewhat rhetorical speech which I have just put into the Church's mouth.

But I did leave something out: I did not mention original sin. For the practical purposes of daily life, this alters the picture sharply. It means that we stand towards sex, as towards other good things, very much as a

precariously-reformed alcoholic stands towards a glass
of wine. We need to be very careful: while recognising
the sacredness of Venus, we must risk hurting her feelings by emphasising her daemonic potential more forcibly than she really deserves.

But that's a sad fact about us, not a fact about her.
Original sin lies in the congenitally damaged soul and
will, not in the body, though it has certain consequences
there of imperfect control, as every man discovers. So
long as we are talking about physical sexuality, it need
not come into the picture.

Any full study of Catholic teachings about sex, theological and historical in scope, would lie beyond my
present purposes, beyond my competence as well. The
interested reader will find that many such studies are
already in existence. Some recent ones need cautious
interpretation, being governed by a desire to modify
those teachings instead of simply exploring them. Of
those that can be recommended without any such qualification, I would choose *Two in One Flesh*[2] for particular
emphasis. Although slightly ponderous in literary and
theological method, it is excellent as a scholar's justification of what I have tried to say—in more rhetorical
language—by way of interpreting 'the mind of the
Church'.

But despite any such citing of scholarly witness, certain doubts will probably remain, though they may
concern habitual attitudes rather than formal doctrine.
How accurately have I interpreted the *effective* 'mind of
the Church'? I offered that outline statement of the

[2] E. C. Messenger, *Two in One Flesh* (London: Sands, 1950).

Catholic message about sex, as it might be put before some pagan or primitive: the reader may feel that it makes a very fine message, but sounds curiously unlike what the Church has actually been saying for these nineteen centuries. Is it perhaps nothing more than my own idea of what the Church *ought* to have been saying?

Many people, if asked to dramatise its actual message—the one that has effectively got across to the majority, within the Catholic fold and elsewhere—would come up with something more like this:

"It seems that the Lord is not going to return in glory as quickly as we had expected and hoped. He wants the human race to carry on for a while longer in this Vale of Tears, presumably in order to provide more candidates for Heaven. That means that there will have to be babies; and that means, I suppose, that there will need to be sexual intercourse.

"Now I can't say that sexual intercourse is an *absolutely* evil thing: as we see from Genesis, it was ordained and commanded by God. But thanks to the Fall, it no longer exists in the form which God ordained and commanded. It was the first consequence of that 'aboriginal catastrophe' to turn the organs of generation into the parts of shame: that's what they are today, and their use—even at the best, even in the fruitful use of marriage—is now a dirty and shameful business, a surrender to animality, a sleep of reason, a kind of squalid madness. I might possibly go too far if I said that this act was always and inherently sinful. But it is at least always, or very nearly always, accompanied by sin—by sin which will be extremely serious if you wallow in the bestial pleasures which it makes possible.

"Most regrettably, I cannot in present circumstances

forbid this ugly thing altogether. It does serve a useful purpose, after all. But it is clear that anybody who aspires to priesthood or real holiness will have absolutely nothing to do with it, and will need to take a vow in that sense: it is clear also that those for whom the act is technically lawful will need to exercise extreme restraint. They must be allowed to perform it, I suppose, but sparingly, only within marriage and for strictly reproductive purposes, in full awareness that they are playing with fire and making themselves vulnerable to Satan at his most powerful. Any different or further use of the reproductive organs—such as might involve the frustration of their reproductive function, or be undertaken for mere pleasure, or outside marriage, or between people of the same sex or in other perverted versions—will be an abomination before God and man and will incur the just vengeance of Heaven.

"It is not for us to question the mysterious dispositions of God. But I cannot help wondering why he should have ordained and commanded anything so disgusting, so unworthy of rational and spiritual beings, in the first instance.

"*Venus*? Don't mention that name to me! It stands jointly for two of the vilest things in this wicked world—unbridled lechery, and the worship of idols."

A message in that sense would be very unlike the more enthusiastic and positive though still cautionary message which I outlined earlier. We can differentiate between the two in various ways. We might ask, for example, which of the two appeals more strongly to ourselves. Alternatively, we might ask which of the two is more objectively realistic: our own preferences may possibly be somewhat skewed or warped.

But for my present purposes, the important question is a different one. Which of the two comes closer to representing the authentic mind of the Catholic Church?

That is a question of some subtlety.

Let us speak for convenience of the Positive Message and the Negative Message, remembering always that the Positive Message includes a strongly cautionary element and that the other was never *totally* negative. It was never the Catholics, it was always the heretics who went the whole hog and said (in effect) that sex was of the Devil's making.

The contradiction between the two messages is not absolute. Within limits, it resembles the seeming contradiction between the optimist who says that a certain bottle is half-full of wine and the pessimist who says that it is half-empty. Both are right: the difference between the two is a matter of temperament. Alternatively, we might say that these are only two different messages because they are about two different subjects: the one is about the sacred Venus, the other is about the daemonic Venus. Both locate her within the realm of the sacred, however furiously the Negative Message pushes her towards the daemonic pole of that realm: neither suggests that she is profane and can be handled as we choose.

Nor must we suppose that 'very dangerous when abused' means the same thing as 'inherently evil', however obsessively it may be said. One can harp single-mindedly upon dangers where one perceives no further evil at all. Imagine that a man's work involves the handling of explosive or radio-active or otherwise dangerous materials. The walls will be plastered with warning notices, he will need to be thinking of safety-precautions all the time, his employers—dreading accidents and litigation—will nag incessantly. Negative utterances will fill the air. But none of them will reflect adversely upon the materials handled. It will be taken for granted on all sides that they fulfil some useful purpose and are in that sense 'good': there will be no need for notices and reminders in that sense. An overall impression of one-sided and obsessive negativism may thus be given, but misleadingly.

The Church always spoke pastorally in the first instance, and only then philosophically; and it might be argued that the Negative Message was what people needed to hear, even though it did not amount to the whole truth. Natural man has certain deep ambivalences about sex, and I shall return to these later, to his widespread fears of a simply daemonic Venus. But in general and in the most obvious sense, he is keen: he goes in for sex most energetically. In so far as it is a good thing, he hardly needs to be informed of the fact: in so far as there are dangers, these will be the main preoccupation of those who care for him.

But no such arguments can be pressed very far. Even a slight acquaintance with the vast corpus of Christian and Catholic writing, from the Fathers of the Church onwards and right into this present century, will make it clear that the exact note of my Negative Message has been struck clearly and consistently and by many, including some of the most respected theologians, and not only when they were writing pastorally and needed to warn the sinner in forcible language. They often struck exactly the same note when writing more philosophically, attempting something in the way of an overall balanced appraisal.

Thus and otherwise, a beautifully simple belief has gained very wide acceptance. *The Catholic Church is against sex*. It's as simple as that, people think, with just the one grudging exception that has to be made if human life is to continue.

For many, some version of that belief amounts to an entirely obvious fact of history, as when one scholar—writing of D. H. Lawrence—says "I take it for granted that Christianity does depreciate sexuality, or at most make reluctant concessions to it; and that Lawrence was right in believing this, wherever else he was wrong; and that the Chestertonian (and post-Chestertonian) trick of representing Christianity as a robustly Rabelaisian sort of faith is a vulgar propagandist perversion."[3] Justice is hardly done there to either Chesterton or Rabelais, and the witness of Lawrence is decidedly questionable. Even so, many people would regard the general point there made as a self-evident one, especially where the mind of Catholic Christianity is concerned.

We can see why: that is to say, the factors that have caused this delusion to prevail are obvious enough and have frequently been studied. I shall consider three of them briefly, turning then to a fourth factor which has received insufficient attention so far.

One key factor is a tendency to confuse the mind *of* the Church with the minds of people *in* the Church. Ideally, the two should coincide precisely: in practice, they can differ substantially. The pattern of widespread and influential thinking *in* the Church can be affected by ideas

[3] Graham Hough, *The Dark Sun* (London: Duckworth, 1956), 246 n.

and sentiments that have little to do with the mind *of* the Church, and may indeed be sharply at variance with it. Good Catholics can pick such things up, perhaps uncritically and even unconsciously, from the currently dominant climate of opinion, which is always a powerful thing.

Marxism is now a case in point. We may reject it consciously and be influenced by it none the less, even to the point of a certain internal stress and schizophrenia.

During the early centuries of the Church and later too, thinking of the dualistic or Gnostic or Manichaean sort exercised an influence comparable to that exercised nowadays by Marxism. Logically speaking, it was quite as incompatible with Christianity as Marxism is. Its roots were hellenic and oriental, not scriptural or apostolic, and it contradicted the very first words of the Bible and the Creeds, attributing inherent evil to this world and our bodily condition. But people are seldom altogether logical, and their emotional and imaginative patterns can often be at variance with their set beliefs. In our time, many good Christians are so filled with understandable compassion for the poor and with dislike for Big Business that they drift remarkably far— emotionally and imaginatively speaking—in the Marxist direction: to hear them talk about political and economic matters, one would suppose that they actually *were* Marxists by full conviction. And in very much the same way, many early Christians—including some of those rightly seminal theologians whom we call the Fathers of the Church—were so very conscious of the evils of this life and the need for asceticism that they spoke in something very closely resembling a dualistic or Manichaean idiom. Their emotional and imaginative life was deeply coloured by something quite alien to their Faith and quite incompatible with it.

This is understandable. Part of what those alien cults emphasised bore a superficial but strong resemblance to an important part of what the Lord had said and what his Church must always say. There is a certain sense in which the Christian must always 'despise the world', in which he must live 'in the spirit' and free himself from the shackles of 'the flesh': death, the defeated ending of all bodily hopes, must always seem to him a blessed release, a liberation, a journey—if all goes well—to his true Home. This is by no means the whole of how he needs to see his present condition. But it is one part of his Gospel truth; and if his times are such as to suggest earthly doom and apocalyptic disaster, or if he is fastidious or pessimistic by temperament, it will be the part upon which he seizes most firmly.

So long as he keeps his feet upon the firm ground of dogma, little harm will follow. He will see the creation of this world, and his own birth in particular, as a matter for gratitude, not as some colossal mistake or misfortune. He will remember that the Creator of all things is loving and good, not Satanic, the consequent enigma of theodicy being resolved on the Cross: he will remember the Incarnation that precedes the Cross, and that mix-up of the Godhead with flesh will speak to him very pointedly indeed: inescapably though mysteriously, his Creeds will remind him that his body is something that will rise again, eternally and in glory, not something evil that needs to be firmly and finally discarded.

But under pressure from experience and the age, his emotions and his imagination may pull him in another direction. They may suggest to him that the 'world' which needs to be despised and rejected is this lovely planet and everything it carries, instead of the ugly 'world' of contentious human pride, of trend-worship and competitive self-esteem. They may cause him to feel as though the 'flesh' of which St. Paul spoke harshly were the physical body (*soma*) and not the general corruption of our fallen nature (*sarx*). About sex, he may then seem to have two options. He may feel that whereas his soul is divine and incapable of sin, his body is irremediably fixed in the evil world of Satan or the *demiourgos*, so that nothing done by it can have spiritual consequences for good or for ill. Alternatively, he may come to see sexual intercourse as a wholly daemonic thing, partly as an act of the corrupt flesh and not of the pure spirit, and perhaps also because it commonly leads to birth, to a further entrapment of God in Satan's prison of clay. Either way, he will look upon it with hatred.

Where such dualistic or Manichaean theologies were fully embraced, in frank opposition to Catholic Christianity, each of those two options—of total 'permissiveness', and of total horrified chastity—was in fact recommended and followed. But among the more orthodox and until very recent times, the former option seemed too obviously un-Christian to gain much recommendation. That left the latter. It was equally un-Christian, in fact, to say or suggest that God did something disgusting when he invented sex. But to the emotional and imaginative apprehensions of an ascetic, surrounded by people whose sexual behaviour was very disgusting indeed, it will not have seemed so obviously un-Christian.

This (I suggest) is how we ought to understand that radical antipathy to sex which we find in some of the Fathers, notably in St. Jerome and—although his is a far more complicated case—St. Augustine. "Without pursuing at the moment its undoubted remoter origins, it is clear that its proximate source is to be found in the oriental-hellenic dualism in which the age was steeped, and which had infected Christian sexual thought even while under condemnation by the Church for its heretical influence in other directions."[4] Although all such dualisms were the Church's enemies from the start and at the rock-bottom level of doctrine, they were not always successfully opposed. They have often managed to infiltrate and so become that most dangerous thing, an enemy within the gates. Thinking of that kind has constantly recurred within Catholicism, though always as a mood, never as formal doctrine: it lurks tiresomely in Catholic minds very much as disease-germs lurk in the mouth and bloodstream of a healthy man—regrettably present, alien and unfriendly, hard to eliminate altogether, but not very harmful unless they get out of control.

From this phenomenon, we can draw two related and useful morals. In the first place, it shows us how careful we must be in regarding the early Church, the Patristic age especially, as an absolute and permanent norm for all Christianity. Anglicans, chronically vague about the nature of the Church and the basis of doctrine, have frequently done so: for them, 'antiquity' follows close behind Scripture as a sure guide, the 'primitive' is the authentic. We Catholics also revere our Founding Fathers and rely heavily upon them. But those early Christians were no less subject to extraneous pressures than we are;

[4] Derrick Sherwin Bailey, *The Man-Woman Relationship in Christian Thought* (London: Longmans, 1959), 48.

and if we relied upon them uncritically, not correcting
them when necessary by other manifestations of the
Church's mind—by Scripture, by defined doctrine, by
long-term liturgical practice—feelings if not doctrines
of the most clearly anti-sexual sort would have to be
deemed authentic and correct. They are certainly 'primitive': however un-Scriptural and un-theological, they
were the fashionable thing in those days, and at some
later periods as well. I shall return later to the sense in
which they are the fashionable thing in our own time.

In the second place, we are here reminded that the
dominant theological mood and trend of some particular
time always needs to be taken with a big pinch of salt. It
may claim an absoluteness which it hardly deserves.
Once again, our present time is a case in point.

The idea that Catholicism hates sex gets some further
support from the doctrine of celibacy, and a good deal
more from certain side-effects of its imperfect practice.

The doctrine that celibacy can be a positive vocation for
some and a supremely high one, not merely a repre-
hensible failure to get married, was one of the few
sex-related ideas with which Jesus and his followers will
have startled their original Jewish hearers. It is often
taken in a clearly anti-sexual sense, especially in connection with the Virgin Birth and the perpetual virginity
of Mary, who was always held up as a model for all
womanhood. But here also, that Manichaean or Gnostic
instinct can lead us astray. If we understand the Virgin
Birth too simply in terms of *gnosis* or spiritual meaning,
it will certainly suggest that ordinary birth is a kind of
second-best if not actually deplorable. A more literal,
factual, and down-to-earth approach will enable us to see

the real point more clearly—the fact that the world's Redeemer needed to have a woman for his mother but God for his Father: otherwise he would have been simply a man, the best of all men perhaps, but unable to save us all. A distant analogy is provided by the man who has 'dual nationality' because his father came from one country and his mother from another.

In itself, celibacy carries no anti-sexual implications at all, as will appear from a comparison which I do not intend to be shocking.

Let us consider two young women. One of them, a Catholic, enters a convent and there vows celibacy. The other, brought up in some pagan cult of Venus, either becomes a temple prostitute or else begins her marriage by surrendering her virginity to a temple priest or an anonymous stranger as representing the goddess, according to the ancient practice mentioned in Chapter II.

The moral difference between these two cases is so great that we may overlook the religious element which both have in common. In either case, a young woman's sexuality is seen as having so great a religious importance that it can properly be offered up in sacrifice, to God or to Venus as the case may be. Her virginity is sacred and so needs to be ritually *conferred*: where it can be casually 'lost', as we say nowadays, the suggestion is of a minor carelessness in an unimportant matter, something essentially profane.

So with the sexuality of a priest or monk. If he offers this to God (along with the associated pleasures and comforts and supports that marriage might have given him), he says nothing whatever against it: on the contrary, he locates it clearly within the realm of the sacred. It was always a perfect lamb, the best of one's

flock, that one offered up in sacrifice. If sex were something unclean, its ritual sacrifice would be a kind of
blasphemy.

In the ideal case, the matter will be seen and enacted
like that, with difficulty (sacrifice is hardly supposed to
be easy) but with no further stress. But not all cases are
ideal, and some are distinctly abnormal.

Particular dangers arise when the celibate priesthood is
the chief or only road to education and worldly success,
as has too often been the case in Catholic history: it is
certain in practice that there will then be 'bad vocations'
to this exceptional state. At any time, there is also the
possibility of a man being drawn to the celibate life (or at
least, less sharply repelled by it) because he is naturally
misogynistic; or such feelings may arise within him at
some later stage, stemming from his bad handling of the
combat entailed by any *askesis*. Grace will be helpfully
available, but men do not always respond to grace.
Psychologically therefore at least, certain celibate men of
God can come to see woman as nothing but a temptress,
a devil's snare, a dark and evil thing. (A female celibate
might succumb to a similar neurosis, and in an equally
understandable way: if one attaches any value at all to the
askesis of chastity, there must always be a sense in which
the other sex actually *is* a temptation, except to those
who are homosexual by inclination or pathologically
under-sexed. But where literacy is a male prerogative,
the female side of the matter will not feature very much
in the written record.)

Over much of the Church's history, literacy was in
fact very largely confined not only to the male but to the
celibate male. The record is thus somewhat 'skewed'.
Even in great theologians, even in some who were later
canonised, misogynism can sometimes rise to patho-

logical heights that delight the anti-Catholic controversialist but have nothing to do with the 'mind of the Church'.

The specially-chosen men and women of God have always carried special and heavy burdens. It implies no undermining of the Faith, no disparagement of Catholicism's central wisdom and sanity, to recognise that some of them have carried heavy burdens of neurosis. That's a common thing in our human condition: holiness does not cure it by magic, any more than it heals our other tribulations in the short term. The cross one is given to carry is seldom the cross one would have chosen.

Thirdly, the idea that Catholicism "does depreciate sexuality, or at most make reluctant concessions to it" is fortified—in some minds—by the existence of a strict Catholic morality in such matters.

This is an irrational kind of inference, as we saw in the case of the man who handled dangerous materials and was therefore under a rigorous discipline. 'Dangerous when abused' has nothing whatever to do with 'inherently evil'.

The most obvious parallel here is provided by the Eucharist, the Blessed Sacrament of the altar. This has long been surrounded by controls and prohibitions of the most rigorous kind—by taboos in quantity, if you find that a suitable word. In that connection, the things that you were not allowed to do were numerous and far-reaching: unless you were ritually designated as a priest or sub-priest, for example, a Sacred Person, you were not allowed even to touch the altar vessels, the chalice and paten.

In all this, the psychologist might be disposed to

see a supreme instance of compulsive or obsessive behaviour: the student of comparative religion will speak
more gently, seeing there a typical instance of how men
naturally respond to the extremely sacred.

A neutral observer might hesitate between these two
interpretations. But he would go far astray if he inferred
that Catholics depreciated the Eucharist, or at most
made reluctant concessions to it.

At least three extraneous factors have thus given some
plausibility to the idea that the mind of the Church is
essentially hostile to sex. There is that old tendency for
Catholic minds to be infected by alien germs of the
Manichaean kind: there are certain false interpretations
of celibacy, together with certain undesirable side-effects
that it can have in fact: and there are similarly false
interpretations of a moral code that is undeniably exacting. One might be able to think of further factors that
have tended in the same direction.

But those three factors have been present and operative for a long time: they cannot account fully for the
relatively new situation in which we now find ourselves
—a situation in which a supposed negativism about sex is
the *primary* thing alleged against traditional Catholicism.

This new situation is an extraordinary one. The
Catholic Faith is a large and complex thing: there are
countless points at which people can object to it, and
have frequently done so. But in our time, the objections
brought against it show an overwhelming tendency to
be sex-related in one way or another, with some emphasis upon the question of contraception. That, more
than anything else, is what people want to argue about.
Sex has—it seems—become the primary matter at issue

as between the Church and the world, and also as between certain Catholics and the tradition of their own
Church. There is a deep-seated disagreement here, and
also—as I suggested in the Introduction to this book—a
kind of mutual bewilderment. Does the Church hate
sex? If not, why does it make so much fuss about even
the most private and harmless kinds of sexual behaviour?

A new situation indeed, and it calls for a new explanation, over and above the ancient factors that I
have mentioned. I believe that the approach used in
this book, drawing upon the language of comparative
religion rather than that of Catholic theology, will cast
much light upon it.

The nature of this approach ought to be clear enough
by now. By way of taking it a stage further, let us
consider the difference between two possible diagrams
that we might draw upon a sheet of paper. One would be
linear or bi-polar: we can think of a scale, with the
simply good at one end of it and the simply bad at the
other. As long as we are thinking of morality alone, such
a scale would make great sense: with whatever particular
disagreements here or there, we would locate the best
and noblest actions at one end of it and the worst sins and
crimes at the other. If we felt prepared to judge people
morally, we could classify them in this same linear way:
we would put the great saints at one end of the scale and
the vilest sinners at the other, hoping to find ourselves
nowhere worse than at some intermediate point.

It is in terms of such an imagined scale, I suggest,
that many people interpret Catholic attitudes towards
sex and find them mostly negative. Their reasoning
seems clear enough. One naturally speaks of this or
that according to its position on the scale, as seen by

oneself: one speaks in positive terms about whatever
one considers good and negatively about whatever one
considers bad. The Catholics are on record as saying
many negative things about sex: *ergo*, their Church sees
sex as mostly if not totally evil.

But as we saw in Chapter I, a scale of that linear kind
will prove insufficient as soon as we turn from morality
to 'religion', in the broadest sense of that word. There,
we shall need a different diagram, tri-polar or Y-shaped:
we shall need to speak not simply of the good and the
bad, but of the sacred and the daemonic and the profane.

This necessity will be all the greater as soon as we
adopt premises of the most basically Christian sort.
We shall then see all 'being', as such, as good: we
shall attribute evil to nothing at all except the will and
choice of a rational creature that turns against its Maker,
so moving away from all goodness and therefore—as
though by an asymptotic path—towards its own nonbeing. It will then be more meaningless than false to say
that our physical sexuality, or anything else that exists in
the concrete, is evil. But we shall still need to ask
whether it is sacred or profane; and if it is not profane, if
it has substantial importance of the religious kind, we
shall need to be very careful about such choices and
circumstances as may cause its sacredness to assume the
negative mode, to become daemonic.

This may seem like a quibble: if the daemonic is not
evil, what is?

But we need only remember, once again, the man
who worked with dangerous materials, by no means
evil in themselves, yet capable of becoming his worst
enemy at short notice if abused. Beyond this, we should
remember that while Satan is traditionally seen as daemonic in the extreme, his existence was in no way

evil: God hates nothing that he has made. We should also remember the point made earlier, that by our sin and in his judgment, God himself can become (by our choice) the Adversary, in that sense Satanic, in that sense daemonic. This does not mean that he is, or can become, evil: "The fear of the Lord is the beginning of wisdom," but God is not a bloodthirsty ogre.

The daemonic and the evil are wholly distinct concepts, and we can speak of the daemonic Venus without even the faintest implication that sex is a bad thing.

My point is that in matters of sex, all of us—good Catholics included—are going to misunderstand the mind of the Church if we think of social and personal morality alone and fail to think constantly of sacredness and sacrament.

We may come to feel, for example, that Catholic priests have always harped quite disproportionately upon the sexual sins, paying much less attention to other sins that do a great deal more harm; and we may see this as a weakness or folly of theirs. Is it not obviously because, being celibate, they are obsessively and enviously anxious to restrict delights in which they may not share?

In the minds of certain individual priests, doubtlessly: I have met some obvious cases. But the mind of the Church is something else, and one thing needs to be remembered. You and I may perhaps be tempted to a wide variety of sins, and some of these (if committed) will have personal and social consequences of the most visibly evil sort. But unless we go in for Satanism and the Black Mass, there is only one kind of sin which allures us powerfully and constantly and which (if committed) will involve the profanation of a sacrament.

This point has its relevance to the much-disputed

question of contraception. People often suspect that the Church is there speaking in the spirit of my Negative Message and in some such terms as these. "All right: if you must enjoy these filthy pleasures, I suppose you must. But you mustn't enjoy them simply *as* pleasures. If you do enjoy them, I want to see you paying the full natural price for doing so. You may have your fun, but only if, in return, you burden yourselves with babies. You aren't allowed to get something for nothing!"

That would be a grudging attitude indeed—even though there is nothing so very unreasonable in expecting people to pay for their chosen pleasures. But only prejudice will desire to see the Catholic message about contraception in those harsh terms of price and penalty. It can be understood just as naturally, or more so, in terms of sacredness—in terms of what Salvador Dali (a great artist perhaps, an eccentric certainly, and a Catholic) had in mind when he told us that "The only way to make love is as a sacrament".[5]

What follows if we take his words seriously?

Eliade defines a religious act as "an act with a meaning";[6] and if the service of Venus is a religious or sacramental act in any real sense, its meaning is going to be of crucial importance, calling for extreme respect and fidelity at the religious and not only at the moral level.

Subjectively speaking, in the minds of the parties concerned, the act in question may have a variety of different meanings or perhaps none at all. But although great efforts are made to pretend otherwise, it also has an inherent and objective meaning of the clearest sort,

[5] As quoted in *Time* [European edition], (10 November 1980), 64.
[6] Eliade, *Comparative Religion*, 156.

which is "Get pregnant if you can!" on the male side and "Make me pregnant if you can!" on the female side. Sexual intercourse is about babies: as we might say in the vernacular, it is how blokes turn birds into mums. That is not the sum total of what can be said truthfully about it. But it constitutes the prime definition of what we shall be talking about when we go on to say further things about it. In so far as we forget or overlook this primary fact, our further utterances will be phantasmal.

So far, we might almost be speaking of contraception in psychiatric terms, as a schizoid dissociation of act from meaning. Where such a dissociation is positively intended, a moral question arises which is closely analogous to the moral question of lying.[7]

But a question also arises at the deeper level of religion. What we enact and symbolise and therefore mean, in our normal unimpeded love-making as Christians, is the union in God of love with creativity, the fact that his love is creative and his creativity loving, which is what made the Cross necessary in fact and in logic too. Without the Cross, the enigma of theodicy seems irresolvable: the fact of evil makes it impossible for us to see how the Creator can possibly be perfect in both love and power. Our service of Venus therefore lies close to the heart of the Christian and redemptive mystery, not in some outlying region of specialised consequences; and it does so as a matter of fact, not by some analogy, some fanciful resemblance. If the word 'sacrament' means anything at all in this connection, it means that the symbolic is here the actual—that God is actively present in the marital

[7] See my *Honest Love and Human Life* (New York: Coward-McCann, 1979).

bedroom and deeply involved in what happens there. We should not imagine him as watching our loves from afar, in a mood of detached benevolence though with one eye on the rule-book. He's right in there where the action is; and we, on our side, are correspondingly involved with him, more closely than Tantric and similar mysticisms ever supposed.

It's very natural for us to fear such involvement, to run away from the Hound of Heaven; and behind any choice of contraception, there is a similarly natural fear of the Cross, of the suffering that may indeed come upon heavily-burdened parents or upon the child whose life can only be 'sub-standard' in one way or another. But it is important to remember what will be meant and enacted by reason of that choice. In order to avoid the Cross, we shall be separating love from creativity. Our love-making will still have a theological meaning. But this will now be Manichaean instead of Christian: we shall be enacting the faith of those who denied the possibility of any direct relationship between God's love and the existence of this troubled world. The Venus whom we then serve will be daemonic in the rather specialised sense of being heretical or worse.

This is not the only mode in which our choice can invert her sacredness into a daemonism. The possibilities are various. As we saw in Chapter II, paganism had a strong tendency to see the daemonic Venus in terms of violence and blood. Many Christians, professing a faith with an inescapably ascetic side to it, have emphasised her addictive pleasures, not without some cause. But the Catholic tradition only does so in a surprisingly limited way. St. Thomas, for example, speaks most positively of those pleasures. They would have been even greater if our species had been virtuous and sensible enough to remain in the state of innocence:[8] as things are, they remain so excellent that any frigid failure to appreciate them is going to be a moral defect, a *vitium*, rather than a simple misfortune.[9] He still counsels temperance, as with all the pleasures of sense, but with no suggestion at all that such pleasures are evil.

The strongest emphasis, within the Catholic tradition, is upon the daemonic Venus as an enemy of 'reason'. That word can be misleading. We have now come to associate it with the most coldly detached operations of the pure intellect, and if we find it suggested that our love-life ought to be governed by 'reason', we are naturally put off. Should a loving husband, when in action, approximate himself as closely as possible to a computer? Should syllogisms govern the marriage-bed?

But here, as with St. Paul and the corrupt 'flesh', mistranslation leads us astray. When the older writers used that word 'reason', they had in mind what we would call 'sanity'. The evil that they feared from the daemonic Venus resembles the moral evil of drunkenness or the non-moral evil of lunacy: she can blow your mind, she can drive you crazy. There is nothing bad about sex, but it's not so good to be a sex-maniac; and if we had better standards of comparison than other human beings can provide, we would all see that our sexual sanity is—at the best—a more precarious thing than we like to suppose.

This is one of the deeper and less conspicuous points at

---

[8] St. Thomas Aquinas, *Summa Theologica*, I, q. 98, art. 2.
[9] Ibid., II-II, q. 142, art. 1.

issue as between the Church and the present-day world. The Church has always attached a high value to sanity and also to 'reason' in more recent senses of the word, whereas strong cultural pressures of our time operate in the opposite sense, affecting some Catholic minds as Marxism or Manichaeanism can affect them. The widespread hatred of 'reason', in the sense of logically coherent thought, will be a familiar phenomenon to anyone who operates in the field of religious controversy: I have repeatedly come up against it when attempting to grapple with what they call 'liberal' or 'progressive' Catholicism. Elsewhere, there are many who regard it as a great achievement to blow one's mind by drugs and rock music and the like, and the loss or transcendence of what I have here called 'sanity' is precisely the thing aimed at in the popular cult of Zen Buddhism. So with the daemonic Venus. "Rollo May makes an interesting point when he says that the demonic is any natural function which has the power to take over the whole person":[10] Venus can do exactly that, even to the point of making everything else seem uninteresting. This is one sense in which it is true of her daemonic self that all the pagan gods are devilish,[11] and in which de Rougemont observed that love only ceases to be a devil when it ceases to be worshipped as a god.[12]

Few psychotherapists take sex to be an evil thing. But each of them can bear sad witness to the terrors of the daemonic Venus.

[10] Donald Goergen, *The Sexual Celibate* (London: S.P.C.K., 1976), 100. The reference is to May, *Love and Will*, 123.

[11] Psalm 95:5 (Vulgate).

[12] Denis de Rougemont, *Passion and Society* (London: Faber and Faber, 1956), 312.

I am talking chiefly about a problem of communication. When I put my Positive Message into the Church's mouth, I imagined it as being addressed to some pagan or primitive, to whose mind a tri-polar distinction between the sacred and the daemonic and the profane would come more or less naturally. Such a man would get the point, and would not suppose for a moment that the Church was saying anything against sex itself. Even in these later times, even until very recently, it could speak on the presumption that people would have the relevant "ears to hear", and would not understand a Positive Message about sacredness as though it were a Negative Message about nastiness. But no such presumption can now be made. We sometimes hear it said that the modern world is relapsing into paganism, but it is not: it is relapsing into something very different. "A post-Christian man is not a Pagan; you might as well think a married woman recovers her virginity by divorce. The post-Christian is cut off from the Christian past and therefore doubly from the Pagan past."[13]

In our society, therefore, the Church addresses what is almost a new *kind* of human being, barely capable of understanding the language in which earlier generations could be addressed in some confidence of the message getting across in the sense intended. Its task, never easy, has thus become difficult in a new way and may perhaps call for a new idiom: this book is partly meant as an exercise and even a recommendation in that sense. Catholic Christianity was always likely to be rejected by some and accepted very half-heartedly by others,

[13] C. S. Lewis, *De Descriptione Temporum*, an inaugural lecture at Cambridge. As reprinted in *They Asked for a Paper* (London: Geoffrey Bles, 1962), 20.

as we were warned in the Parable of the Sower. But when about sacredness and sex, it now incurs an unprecedented danger of not getting across at all. The very idea of sacredness has been mostly forgotten: in its absence, people subconsciously assume that sex is something profane, or even that it is wholly and simply daemonic, as we shall see in the following chapters. One way or another, they lack "ears to hear": they fail to see what the Church is talking about. All that comes across to them is a warning message of "Lilies that fester smell far worse than weeds", and they interpret this in negative terms alone, as a distrustful condemnation of those flowers. They overlook the tremendous thing that was previously and primarily said, by that same voice, about the lilies of the field in all their glory.

Chapter Four

The Profane City

We are a weird lot, anthropologically speaking, we of the modern post-Christian West. There are many respects in which we differ from the peoples of other times and cultures: our knowledge of the physical universe is so much greater, our technology is so much more advanced, our differentiation of social roles is so much more complex, we are so extraordinarily preoccupied with economics and our 'standard of living'. But we have a further peculiarity, one that lies closer to the heart of human experience. We live as though in a profane universe: the concept of sacredness, so frequently mentioned in these pages because so crucial for most human existence, has practically disappeared from the common life of our society.

Any message about sacredness has therefore become difficult to put across: it tends to be understood as though it were about something else.

This is among the great novelties of our present condition: "the *completely* profane world, the wholly desacralised cosmos, is a recent discovery in the history of the human spirit",[1] and it is perhaps in this rock-bottom sense that we can most usefully describe our society as post-Christian, as post-religious.

[1] Eliade, *Sacred and Profane*, 13.

There are, of course, further senses in which it has that character. It is a commonplace to observe that the last hundred years or so have seen a steady decline of religious belief in most Western countries: fewer people attend public worship, the influence of the churches has become weaker, the priest or minister or rabbi enacts a more limited social role than he once did. Even where some traditional faith is still professed, we often find it professed in a form that has changed beyond all recognition, abandoning its old certainties of doctrine and morality and approximating itself more and more closely to the dominant secular thought of the time.

But it is also a commonplace to point out that the whole truth is not of this kind, especially if we see 'religion' primarily in terms of belief in God and then in terms of morality. God may well have been relegated to the background of many people's lives, to be invoked as an airman uses his parachute, only in the direst kind of emergency. But he is seldom denied altogether and dogmatically: full-blooded atheism is still a rare thing, and cannot always be taken at its face-value even where professed. And as is made clear by every statistical enquiry into the book trade and its sales, 'religion'—in the broadest sense, and with many eccentric variations—is still a subject that interests people profoundly.

As for morality, it's hard to be sure. Are we really so much worse than our forefathers, by Christian standards or any other? We certainly do many things that would have shocked them; but in their time, they also did things that shock us when we read about them. The world's wickedness may seem to be greater than it was, but this may be simply because more of it gets onto the record. We have any amount of hard facts and figures about Now, but much fewer about Then, so that we cannot easily make fair comparisons. It seems plausible to guess that while the patterns of human wickedness, and also of shocked response to it, are subject to incessant variation as between different times and cultures, the percentile incidence of both—as seen by God—may be something like a constant. When the last censorious thing has been said about 'the permissive society' and also about the public acceptance of abortion and nuclear armaments and other such horrors, it is still far from clear that ours is an *exceptionally* wicked generation.

It is at the rock-bottom level of 'religion' that we really are exceptional—that is to say, in respect of this big change, this all-but-universal and (it seems) unprecedented forgetting of sacredness, this mental shift into a wholly profane cosmos.

It is a shift that began a long time ago, perhaps around the beginning of the nineteenth century,[2] and has been progressively consummated ever since. Many have welcomed it, in the name of science and modernity and progress. But it has also aroused various kinds of alarm and regret, sometimes in unexpected quarters and not always for specifically religious reasons. It is possible, we are told by one writer, "to say that the quality of life would improve for many people by a recovery of the sacred, of the 'holy', dimension in their lives. This view could be held by clergy, and even by social scientists, especially those in the Jungian tradition."[3]

[2] See Lewis, *De Descriptione Temporum*.
[3] Robert Bocock, *Ritual in Industrial Society* (London: George Allen and Unwin, 1974), 20.

If the name of Jung is to be invoked at all, the point could be made more forcibly than that. But the motivation behind such sentiments, when not religious, need not be psychological. If we heard a sad cry of "All that is holy is profaned!" we might suppose ourselves to be hearing some churchman's lament over the infidelity of the day. In fact, those are the words of Marx and Engels, writing in the original Communist Manifesto and lamenting the sterilising and desacralising effect which they attributed to bourgeois society.[4]

For my present purposes, the city which Harvey Cox called 'secular' can better be called 'profane'. That's where we mostly live nowadays, in the profane city, even if we live there as dissidents. Our language reflects the fact. The word 'sacred' is still used by particular religious groups, but mostly in a weak and over-simplified sense from which all bi-polarity has departed: it is also used by anthropologists and others who study such groups at home and abroad, but then with the scholar's detachment, with no suggestion of an apprehension shared by the writer. Its wider use is mostly jocular, as when we greet some petty iconoclasm with a cry of "Is *nothing* sacred any more?" 'Profane' has suffered a similar fate: its dominant use is that of a facetiously archaic synonym for words like 'obscene' or 'blasphemous' when applied to language. And in the colloquial English of our time, there is *no* word that corresponds at all closely to *pietas*. 'Piety' has acquired a very different sense: it means little more than 'assiduous devotion', as rather patronisingly seen. This is not at all the same thing

[4] Karl Marx, *Selected Works*, I (London: Lawrence and Wishart, 1942), 209.

as that reverential awe, not unmixed with fear and acted out in ritual, by which men respond most naturally to the sacred.

If such sentiments played any large part in our collective experience nowadays, we would have found some convenient single word for them.

Much has been written about this desacralised quality of our modern world. It is not a quality that reigns absolutely: there are certain points at which the sacred still holds out, and these deserve attention. "To whatever degree he may have desacralised the world, the man who has made his choice in favor of a profane life never succeeds in completely doing away with religious behaviour. . . . even the most desacralised existence still preserves traces of a religious valorization of the world";[5] and Eliade has much to say about the sterile and absurd forms—from Marxism to occultism—taken by the sacred when it still breaks out in the lives of those who wish to deny it altogether.[6]

Even in the profane city, it still breaks out in certain more respectable forms; and these have the illustrative value of particular and limited exceptions to an otherwise all-pervading tendency.

It is significant, for example, that we still go in for behaviour of the ritual or symbolic kind, although in a limited way and often in some self-consciousness.[7] Our forefathers went in for much more of it, and more naturally. "The Pagan and Christian ages alike are ages of what Pausanias would call the *dromenon*, the exter-

[5] Eliade, *Sacred and Profane*, 23.
[6] See ibid., 204–10.
[7] See Bocock, *Ritual*, for a full treatment of this subject.

nalised and enacted idea; the sacrifice, the games, the triumph, the ritual drama, the Mass, the tournament, the masque, the pageant, the epithalamium, and with them ritual and symbolic costumes, *trabea* and laticlave, crown of wild olive, royal crown, coronet, judge's robes, knight's spurs, herald's tabard, coat-armour, priestly vestment, religious habit—for every rank, trade or occasion its visible sign."[8] As against any such enactment of the special and even the sacred, it is our instinct to prefer the casual and spontaneous, with behaviour governed much less by pattern and rite and public symbol, much more by the individual's choice of the moment. Anything in the way of solemn ceremonial is likely to make us feel awkward and embarrassed, as being alien to the spirit of the time, false, lacking in authenticity. Even the enacted splendours of the English Monarchy—the Trooping of the Colour, the State Opening of Parliament, the Coronation—have subtly accommodated themselves to that spirit, in the public mind at least: they are now seen much less as quasi-liturgical enactments of the genuinely believed and much more as quasi-theatrical performances, as mere tourist-spectacles.

But ritual does survive, notably there and in other kinds of association with government. There, it might perhaps be understood in the terms proposed by Durkheim, who gladdened the Marxist heart by defining religion in social terms alone. According to him, while religious sentiments and attitudes are nominally directed towards non-existent 'gods', they do have an underlying object which is really there; and "this reality, which mythologies have represented under so many different

---

[8] Lewis, *De Descriptione Temporum*, 14.

forms, but which is the universal and eternal objective cause of those sensations *sui generis* out of which religious experience is made, is society".[9] This is an absurd reductionism if taken sweepingly, but there is something to it. Even now, despite the observations just made, you are more than likely to feel a lump in your throat when the Queen rides by in her State Coach, preceded and followed by a Sovereign's Escort of the Household Cavalry and saluted by drums and trumpets of the Brigade of Guards; and if you do, it is because the people and past of England are there dramatised before your eyes. 'Society' is a profane thing when you read about it in books of social history and present-day analysis: it is at least capable of becoming the subject of sacred drama.

But there are further and more specifically religious senses in which public ritual can still be an enactment of the sacred and even of some divine attribute, notably but not only when it involves government. In brute fact, government is identified and defined by its unchallenged possession of coercive power, and every particular government has its origin in some violent seizing of the power, perhaps in the very distant past. But it nearly always claims some higher and more sacred legitimacy for itself, with or without the use of explicitly religious language. The Japanese Emperor is or was the Son of Heaven, and British sovereigns reign "by the grace of God"; the will and destiny of the German *Volk* was mystically embodied in Hitler; Communist tyrants make an exactly similar claim for themselves and the Party; democratic leaders fight like mad to get to the top and there throw their weight about most profanely, while

[9] Durkheim, *Religious Life*, 418.

swearing all the time that they are only the humble instruments of a strange entity called 'the will of the people'; and most astonishingly, the suckers commonly fall for such talk, consenting thereby to all manner of folly and wickedness.

But the suckers are not entirely wrong. All power is of God, as the Lord observed to Pilate, and every kingdom is an ectype or derivative of the Kingdom: anyone who holds power among men is ritually enacting the divine omnipotence in a human version. This does not mean that he is free before God and man to do whatever he likes, but very much the reverse: it is a circumscription, not a liberty. But it does mean that the rest of us look upon him with a certain awe, naturally and in a way rightly, giving this some ritual enactment. A king, as such, is a Sacred Being, even if he is a grotesquely wicked man as well. Shakespeare's history plays are full of the consequent tensions, which are not fully resolved by desacralising a Monarchy into a Presidency.

Further public rituals can carry implications of the same sort. In most countries, for example, the law is still a somewhat ceremonious affair, having its own hieratic diction and calling for robes and dignity and respect: is this because men are there attempting, however imperfectly, to enact the justice of God? And in our universities, on great occasions at least, one can still see scholars whose learning may well be wholly profane, but who none the less assume a version of ecclesiastical dress and rite for its solemn celebration: are they perhaps enacting a further attribute of God, his wisdom? We might even say something similar of armies. A grand military parade is a show of strength among other things, and sometimes a way of intimidating the populace: it also serves to promote group-solidarity and morale among the soldiers, and if it generates a positive response in the spectator, this will be partly a matter of simple patriotism. But something else will be involved as well: it will elicit a kind of awe, distinctive in quality, not paralleled by even the most splendid of civilian displays. Could this be because, in its own kind of pomp and circumstance, an army enacts the sacredness of its primary business, which is death?

In our time, there are always ambiguities in such public enactments of the sacred: some people equate all ceremony with falsity and fuss, calling for brisk functional practicality instead. But there is one such public enactment of which this is hardly true at all: it is such a perfect instance of what the sacred is and how it affects people, under some aspects at least, that it might almost be used to introduce that concept in the first instance.

An English writer needs to handle it with delicacy: I shall do so by means of an anecdote, the truth of which I do not guarantee.

It seems that in the course of Allied co-operation during the Second World War, it became necessary to transfer certain small mechanical parts from a British to an American warship at sea. The parts in question were first wrapped in oily rags and then tied up in some kind of package for transfer across the heaving waters.

Now all navies use a great many flags, for identification and signalling and such purposes; and it is or was the thrifty practice of the Royal Navy, when its various flags become tattered and worn out, to give them further usefulness as rags instead of just throwing them away. So when the Americans received their package, they found that the mechanical parts within it had been wrapped in oily rags which turned out—upon inspection—to be the tattered remains of a Union Flag (I am told that 'Union Jack' is a solecism).

They were shocked, horrified, appalled. How *could* these British sailors treat their own most Sacred Object in such a profane manner? They themselves would never have subjected Old Glory to such a humiliation!

This was the high comedy of misunderstanding. All countries venerate their national flags, but in different degrees and different ways. In America—which is the name of a country, but also (in some ways) the name of an ideology and almost a religion—the national flag is treated with quite exceptional seriousness. It is very much a Sacred Object, and its handling is therefore governed by a strict code of para-liturgical behaviour called 'Flag Etiquette'. One often sees this in print: I don't suppose it has the force of Federal law, but it is followed as strictly as though it had, or more so. It provides (among other things) a kind of funeral rite for the disposal of Old Glory, once the individual flag has worn out and become unusable. There are various options, but these very definitely do not include its relegation to the profane purposes of the engineer.

It is different with the British. They also, or most of them, venerate their national flag. But they do so less intensely—partly because their patriotism seldom has those ideological and quasi-religious overtones, and partly because it is to the Monarchy that they traditionally attribute the sacral and symbolic quality which Americans (having no Monarch) concentrate upon their flag.

Hence the misunderstanding that arose on that windy

occasion at sea. The British had treated as profane something which the Americans expected everybody to treat as sacred: they had acted permissively in an area which —on the American view—called for controlled and ritual behaviour.

One can imagine a highly improbable situation in which the converse shock might have been given—as, for example, if one of those American sailors had been ushered into the presence of His Majesty King George VI and had there spoken and behaved as casually as he would in any other company.

We are all conscious of the obvious sense in which a king is only a man and a flag is only a piece of cloth. If we attribute a kind of sacredness to either, we do so arbitrarily and by convention. Given a different twist of history, somebody other than George VI might have been King of England during World War II: the country might even have been a republic. The American flag also might have taken some totally different pattern: in fact, that country's Sacred Object did not need to be a flag at all. Something wholly un-flag-like might have been for the Americans what St. Stephen's Crown is for Hungarians.

If we look around for something more universal and perhaps more objective in the way of sacredness, still apprehended as such, we shall need to turn from public life to an area which is more private though still social: we shall find the clearest example in Death.

This, more than anything else, has resisted the process of desacralisation: here at least, all men see a *mysterium tremendum et fascinans* and respond to it accordingly—that is, by ritual. There is a brutally clear sense in which the dead body—unless we propose to use it as a fertiliser or for medical research, or to eat it for purposes of magic or nutrition—is mere refuse or garbage. But no known society has ever treated it as such: even among the crudest primitives, even among the most hard-boiled materialists, its disposal has to be a matter of ceremony.

This instinct is so universal as to be used as a test of humanity. Ancient bones are sometimes discovered, such as may or may not be fully human: if there are traces of anything like a funeral rite, these are regarded as clinching the matter. All men see death as sacred, and I have already suggested a possible link between this fact and the ceremonial of an army: it is therefore argued (with slightly questionable logic) that if certain archaic beings did see death as sacred, they must have been human beings.

Funeral rites fall into a wider class, one that has received much anthropological and social study. There are at least two great moments of transition in any human life, birth and death, and there are usually a few others as well—the attainment of adult status, marriage outstandingly, and perhaps the adoption of some new mode of living, some new role in society. It would be more than a pun to say that these moments are universally seen as momentous, as sacred, calling for celebration in 'rites of passage'. Such rites are partly impetratory, concerned with individual and social well-being in the new condition or status—with the safety and health of the baby, with the fertility of a marriage, and with the next-world fate of the dead. But they also recognise the sacredness of life itself and heighten the sacredness of those key moments within it, the public awareness of that sacredness as well.

Even among our least religious selves, such rites still continue, and with at least some memory of their sacral meaning. "In Western society the large number of people whose adherence to their religion is merely nominal nevertheless set store by the performance of ritual on three occasions—at birth when a new person enters society, at marriage, and at death when a person leaves it. Such people, we may suppose, are not greatly concerned with the spiritual effect of these rites: yet the fact must reflect a general feeling that these events ought to be in some way sacralized."[10] People thus enter a church for a christening or a wedding or a funeral who would not enter it otherwise, even if they enter it split-mindedly, seeing the occasion in social rather than in sacral terms. We often see them looking awkward in the church, during the ritual, but relaxing and beginning to enjoy themselves at the party afterwards, even if it is a funeral party.

Sacredness is thus still apprehended in our rites of passage, but more and more tenuously. Even the rites themselves get minimised. When marriage is given the full treatment, its traditional symbolism—of virginity in the bride's white garments, of permanence in the words spoken, and of hoped-for fertility in the rice or confetti thrown at the happy couple—is such as to generate mixed responses nowadays: many people prefer to settle for something simpler and less pointed, even for a purely civil rite in that supremely profane place, a government office. Death itself gets desacralised in some degree. Even the poorest Victorians did their best in the way of

[10] Lucy Mair, *An Introduction to Social Anthropology* (Oxford: Clarendon Press, 1965), 207.

tremendous funeral panoply, with black-plumed horses and every possible adjunct of a great occasion, and then with a rigorous observance of mourning, which involved close restrictions upon clothing and behaviour over a long period. We no longer externalise our grief so lavishly, and this may be unwise of us: strong feelings can fester when bottled up.

One curious thing, differentiating us from most earlier societies, is our lack of an initiation-rite for the sacralisation of maturity. Such rites were always deeply religious. "This initiation is a long series of ceremonies with the object of introducing the young man into the religious life: for the first time, he leaves the purely profane world where he passed his first infancy, and enters into the world of sacred things. Now this change of state is thought of, not as a simple and regular development of pre-existing germs, but as a transformation *totius substantiae*—of the whole being. It is said that at this moment the young man dies, that the person he was ceases to exist, and that another is instantly substituted for it. He is re-born under a new form."[11] All this can be seen as a pre-Christian foreshadowing of baptism. But we, Catholics and Protestants alike, are mostly baptised in infancy, and we seldom give Confirmation the social importance that the Bar-Mitzvah has among the Jews: we have no effective rite of passage by which the young person assumes upon maturity "a new mode of being, that which is proper to an adult—namely, that which is conditioned by the almost simultaneous revelation of the sacred, of death and of sexuality".[12]

[11] Durkheim, *Religious Life*, 39.

[12] Mircea Eliade, *Myths, Dreams, and Mysteries* (London: Fontana, 1970), 199.

Do we thereby deprive our adolescents? Primitive initiation-rites tended to be painful and generally traumatic. But they had their psychological value at least; and if there is a distinctive 'problem of modern youth', this may be partly because we prolong childhood indefinitely, never ending it with ritual decisiveness. It might be socially advantageous if we could re-establish some clear-cut rite of passage, before which one has all the freedom and irresponsibility of a child, and after which one carries the full burden of being a grown-up. In practice, while we allow the attainment of legal majority to provide the excuse for a nice rowdy party, we do little else to meet this real psychological and social need.

The trouble is, of course, that it's primarily a need of initiation into the sacred, and into death and sexuality as seen in sacred terms; and we cannot give our young people what we do not possess ourselves.

Ours is not, therefore, a *totally* profane city. Within it, there is still a certain apprehension of the sacred, a memory of it at the very least, some public and private enactment of it as well, in ritual and perhaps otherwise.

But all such manifestations are increasingly marginal: we have to look for them, we find them in specialised activities and exceptional moments. Only for a few is any strong sense of the sacred woven into the texture of daily life. Even in continuing rites and ceremonies, its presence is often merely vestigial. There is certainly a big difference between a formal dinner-party and a casual snack: similar acts of eating get ritualised in the one case but not in the other. But this could only be called a religious difference by an extreme application of Durkheim's analysis.

In general and with Death as the primary exception, feelings of awe and *pietas*, as before some *mysterium tremendum et fascinans*, are—for all practical purposes— simply absent from most characteristically modern lives. The imagination may still remain sensitive, touched at times by something beyond all understanding:

> Just when we're safest, there's a sunset-touch,
> A fancy from a flower-bell, some one's death,
> A chorus-ending from Euripides,
> And that's enough for fifty hopes and fears,—
> The grand Perhaps;[13]

but such moments are more often solitary than shared, and they can be bracketed off comfortably as 'aesthetic experience', rewarding but subjective, unrelated to the practical business of daily life. Even in such attenuated versions, the sacred has no place there.

One might expect things to be radically different among religious people, who still abound. They have their differences, as we all know. But are they not united in retaining a deep sense of the sacred even when others forget it? Is it not by reason of this that we identify them, specifically, as *religious* people? Will we not find them fighting a stubborn rearguard action against the desacralising tendency of the time, united in that rock-bottom cause if divided elsewhere?

The curious thing is that we find no such unanimity in fact. About that rock-bottom question, we find religious people—Christians very much included—quite as deeply divided as they are about any further questions of faith or morals or worship. Some of them, perhaps the

[13] Robert Browning, *Bishop Blougram's Apology*.

great majority, still retain a deep sense of the sacred as against the profane. But others—a minority, no doubt, but a vocal and influential minority—are as hostile to that dichotomy as any materialist could possibly be, although for reasons that are claimed to be unlike his. Many of them want Christianity itself to be desacralised, Christian worship in particular.

Here is an instance of how they think, in sharp contrast with how people thought in the Christian past and in the pagan past as well.

Consider the act of entering a church or temple, a holy place. Primitive man tended to see sacredness in particular concentrations, in hierophanies; and among these, there would usually be places or buildings of notable holiness. This instinct was carried over into historical Christianity, so that Eliade could see this act of entering a church as a 'rite of passage' in itself, marked —in traditional Catholic practice—by the taking of holy water, the sign of the Cross, and genuflection. Thus we pass from the profane world into the sacred world: the church's door or threshold is "the limit, the boundary, the frontier that distinguishes and opposes two worlds— and at the same time the paradoxical place where those worlds communicate, where passage from the profane to the sacred world becomes possible".[14] That passage effects a discontinuity from ordinary life and a corresponding change in our behaviour: we adopt distinctive postures, even distinctive facial expressions, we communicate as little as possible and then in whispers.

Here as in so many other matters, Catholic practice goes along with natural human instincts while also trans-

[14] Eliade, *Sacred and Profane*, 25.

forming them: Protestant practice has done the same thing in varying degrees.

But this sense of the church building as 'sacred space' is listed by one celebrated modern divine among the things which will now have to go, along with the wider sacredness of worship in general. "The marks of the liturgy in future", says the author of *Honest to God*, "are likely to be informality, flexibility and continuity with ordinary life-style, so that there is no forced sense of stepping out of one world and into another, no compulsory cultural circumcision as one 'enters church'."[15]

It is as though Dr. Robinson were there writing with Eliade's words in mind. He recognises that possibility of two worlds and—in the half-jocular word "circumcision"—of the transition between them being a 'rite of passage'; and as is clear from the context, he considers it highly desirable, not just "likely", that this discontinuity, this particular enactment of the distinctively sacred, should at least be minimised in the Christian worship of the future if not wholly absent from it. He sees it as a bad thing.

His words "forced" and "compulsory" carry a further implication, an important and very questionable one. They suggest that this proposed desacralisation will be a matter of enhanced liberty, of clerically-imposed shackles being broken at last. In fact, like many so-called liberations, it will need to be imposed. The sense of 'sacred space', and of sacredness in general, is what comes naturally to religious man, pagan or Christian, and it easily runs to superstitious excess. One might

[15] John A. T. Robinson, *Christian Freedom in a Permissive Society* (London: S. C. M. Press Ltd., 1970), 192.

argue that it needs to be disciplined by ecclesiastical authority. But this would hardly be the liberation that Dr. Robinson's words suggest.

Thus and otherwise, he illustrates a powerfully de-sacralising trend in present-day Christian theology, affecting worship and much else as well. It is in exactly that sense, and in response to no pressure from the faithful at large, that Catholic worship has recently undergone so marked a transformation. The Mass had been seen and celebrated for centuries as a supremely sacred thing. It was a sacrifice, a making-holy, before it was anything else: everything about it spoke of the sacred and was designed to elicit responses of awe—the ancient and inflexible ritual, the hieratic Latin, the slow solemn chant, the anointed priest railed off and lifted high in the inviolable sanctuary. Whatever else this was, it was certainly 'sacred drama' of the highest order, and could have an extremely strong effect even upon the unbeliev-ing spectator. But recent changes have altered the picture radically, especially when (as often) they go far beyond anything officially authorised. It is now usual to speak not of a sacrifice but of that relatively profane thing, a meal in common. The vernacular has mostly replaced the Latin, and—for English-speaking people at least—in an idiom of almost studied banality: the rite itself is more flexible, more casual, and its music will often be 'profane' in every possible sense: the priest's function is largely shared by laypeople, and the priest himself will be down among the congregation as one of them. Some people prefer to call him 'the president of the assembly', since the word 'priest' has acquired inescapably sacral overtones. If the church itself is new, it will often be such as to suggest an airport lounge rather than the temple of an ancient cult: if old, it may have been given some clumsy and discordant modification in that sense. Countless further changes, most of them small and individually unimportant, add up to an overall suggestion that the real object of present-day Catholic worship is profane contemporaneity and experienced togetherness.

All this goes far beyond the field of liturgy. Priests and nuns used to dress sacrally: many of them now do so in a lesser degree, or only upon occasion, or not at all. Where we once heard reverential talk of 'Our Blessed Lady' and 'The Holy Father', we now hear curt mention of 'Mary' and 'Wojtyla'. The preacher, once concerned with divine mysteries and the salvation of souls, is now likely to concentrate upon the secular problems of the day: many bishops seem more anxious to go along with the trend and say acceptable things than to enact any more sacredly exalted and arduous conception of their office.

The list of such developments, among Catholics and in the other Christianities, could be a long one: although various in form and importance, they add up to a consistent playing-down of that distinction—emphasised by practically all humanity and by all previous Catholicism—between the sacred and the profane.

To avoid misunderstanding, let me here dissociate myself from those Catholics who over-dramatise this tendency into a kind of apostasy, and who therefore go off into such *ecclesiolae* as that of Archbishop Lefèbvre. I am not here concerned, in fact, with any kind of value-judgment: I only want to point out that this tendency exists and is relevant to the practical difficulty of communication in any matter concerning the sacred. If we speak of sacredness in any connection whatever, we shall naturally expect our message to fall on deaf ears where the materialist is concerned: we have known this for a long time. But in so far as the profane city now includes a profane or secularised Church, we must now—and for the first time—expect to find some Christian ears comparably deaf, or at least unwilling to hear, and perhaps even hostile. The message may fail to get across, or even be resisted, where it might have expected a welcome.

I shall return later to the wider aspects of this tendency. It might be deemed self-contradictory and absurd. People seldom call for hot ice or chaste prostitution: what can we make of this call for a desacralised religion, a desacralised Christianity?

But two observations may be pertinent at this point. One of them anticipates the subject of the next chapter. The call for a desacralised Christianity goes along with the call for a desacralised Venus: there is a visible tendency for the same people to be active in both causes, which is at least consistent of them.

It should also be noted that there is a strong humanitarian and psychological case against all desacralisation as such. The sacred attracts us but it repels us too, perhaps more powerfully, and we may feel disposed to get rid of it altogether. But we shall pay a high price for doing so. Subjectively at least, human nature sees the sacred as the supremely real, and any "resistance to the sacred carries with it, in the perspective of existential metaphysics, a *flight from reality*".[16] Any rejection of the sacred is going to be experienced as a rejection of reality and therefore of

[16] Eliade, *Comparative Religion*, 460: emphasis in original. See above, 24.

meaning. An American writer has made a close study[17] of the more desacralised kind of worship in its actual operation, and he has little difficulty in showing—on the basis of much hard evidence—that a worship so transformed soon ceases to be worship in fact and becomes an essentially pointless kind of activity, unable to hold people's interest for very long.

The validity of this psychological principle extends far beyond the field of worship: the desacralised naturally tends to become the unreal, the meaningless, and so to make for despair.

The secular or profane city is a place with a high suicide-rate.

[17] James Hitchcock, *The Recovery of the Sacred* (New York: Seabury Press, 1974).

Chapter Five

Venus Desacralised

Nietzsche said that if God is dead, anything is permitted. He had a good point there, even though he expressed it in somewhat perverse and paradoxical terms.

One particular application of that principle might be expressed as "If Venus has lost her divinity, anything of the physically sexual kind is permitted." It seems that a great many people now make that inference, mostly at the subconscious level but—given the premise—correctly, so providing the 'permissive society' with its theoretical basis.

This seems to me the best interpretation of a development that is too often seen in moral terms alone. It is of course a commonplace to speak of the 'permissive society', as established by a recent 'sexual revolution'; and while such things doubtlessly get exaggerated by selective reporting, they are not mere fantasies. But it would be unrealistic to understand them in terms of simple hedonism, or even in terms of some new and universally lax sort of moral philosophy. In some quarters, there does of course prevail a simple *Playboy* philosophy of "Do as you please and have a good time, so long as you don't hurt other people." But in other quarters, you can find a similarly prevalent philosophy that reaches exactly the same conclusion as regards physical sexuality, but is moralistic and even puritanical elsewhere. Talk to the relevant people about social injustice and the arms race, and they will reply in terms of the loftiest moral indignation: observe their manner of living, and you will often find them embracing Holy Poverty in an almost Franciscan manner, by way of reaction from the affluent consumer-society and its wasteful greed. You may perhaps suspect such people of a certain self-righteousness, but not of any general antinomianism: in these other matters, they 'bear witness' in a sense which every good Christian should applaud. And this sound moralism of theirs extends into certain sex-related fields: about the psychological, personal, and relational aspects of our sexual behaviour, they will speak most exactingly. It's only the physical that seems unimportant to them.

Later in this chapter, I shall offer a few illustrations of all this. What I want to emphasise, at this point, is the fundamentally religious nature of the change that has led to this new outlook. The traditionally Christian code of sexual morality was always burdensome and was never obeyed very perfectly. But on the whole, people saw the point of it: they retained the basic apprehension which caused the pagan to see Venus as a goddess and was consummated in the sacramental doctrine of *matrimonium*. As the general sense of sacredness grew weaker, however, this particular kind of sacredness dropped out of sight, and with it, the whole point of that ancient code. Deprived of its point, that code naturally came to seem like nothing more than a mere hang-up, an inhibitory neurosis—something from which we needed, and have largely achieved, a simple liberation.

This diagnosis of the change in question is—I suggest—

not so much plausible as tautological. The profane is, by definition, that which has no religious importance, calls for no *pietas*, and can be handled in any way that seems convenient and advantageous. People are never permissive about anything which they apprehend as sacred. To advocate permissiveness in the handling of our physical sexuality is to say that Venus is no longer a goddess.

Her desacralisation is, in fact, one of the most conspicuous phenomena of our time, an outstanding instance of the wider tendency which I considered in the previous chapter. Living in the profane city, we do at least remember what sacredness was: we still apprehend it in Death, and—more precariously—elsewhere. But most of us keep it or its memory in one mental compartment and physical sex in another, as though the two were mutually irrelevant. We still revere 'love' most deeply, though often with insufficient attention to the crucifying complexity of that word. But for most of us, the genital and especially the female functions have become wholly profane.

A simple social experiment will illustrate this. Religious feelings are commonly respected, even among those who do not share them. Speak in suitably mixed company about God, Christ, the Church, the hope of salvation, and worship: people will know that you are speaking of things that are sacred, to you at least, and will usually respond accordingly, with a somewhat embarrassed kind of deference. But they will be startled and perhaps shocked if you then continue, in the same tone of voice, to speak not of sexual morality but of physical sex in itself. They don't think of that as a religious kind of subject.

What remains of Venus, once we have stripped this great and frightening goddess of her divinity?

One partial answer is obvious enough. What most certainly remains is a kind of satisfaction, a physical pleasure in the first instance but offering further rewards as well, psychological and relational in nature. Venus thus becomes assimilated into the pattern of our other satisfactions as currently understood: she shows a marked tendency to become a consumer-good, an element in that 'high standard of living' which we have come to expect and take for granted in an affluent society.

Affluence is, of course, a recent and a definitely precarious thing. During its thirty years or so of prevalence, we have tended to make an unsustainably rapid consumption of goods and services into our *summum bonum* in this life, often on the economically absurd assumption that very high consumption-levels can be claimed as a matter of right and secured by coercion, no matter what the corresponding production-levels may be. This is what we have in mind when we talk and agonise and fight over our precious 'standards of living', an expression that might conceivably be used in some loftier sense, and it offers an outstanding instance of our society's collective departure from the words of Jesus,[1] its 'post-Christian' quality. Economic anxiety ought to be left to the people who don't know about God: in the present climate of world-wide depression (I write in October, 1981) it seems increasingly unlikely to find positive resolution.

For a great many of us, sex—having been desacralised—

[1] Mt 6:25–34.

has fallen into exactly that pattern of affluent consumerism: it has become one of the satisfactions that we are entitled to demand and to *have*, just as we suppose ourselves entitled to demand and have steaks and colour television and all the other profane blessings of wealth. Regular and satisfactory sex, in any preferred version, has become an integral part of our rightly and deservedly high standard of living. Look at the bookshops. They offer you much advice on how to be a successful consumer. There, on the shelves, you will find a number of handsomely-produced and richly-illustrated volumes on how to get the most out of your cooking: others, on how to get the most out of your car, or your expensive holiday abroad. And in just the same way, further along the shelves, you will find further books that tell you (also with illustrations) how to get the most out of your sex-life, how to consume a high-quality product in this area also: here's how to choose the meat, here's what to do with it, here's how to season it and how to vary it, so avoiding monotony. One such book, a best-seller, is called *The Joy of Sex*; and its very revealing sub-title is *A Gourmet Guide to Love-Making*—an expression which clearly brackets your 'sex-partner' with some epicure's dish. Or consider the similarly revealing expression 'having sex' with somebody. You *have* a steak, you *have* a cocktail, you *have* a big cigar; and in just that way, sex is something that you *have*, in your capacity as a consumer.

It differs from other consumer-goods, of course, in that it doesn't necessarily cost anything. Even so, this way of looking at poor Venus can find expression in quasi-economic terms. "The fact that sex is pleasurable, easily available, free, and time-consuming, is very important for the cybernated new world, over-saturated with leisure, that we are about to enter. America and Western Europe may be in the vanguard of the generally affluent society. But sexual affluence is descending like manna from heaven on most of the world, with the control of conception, the increase of men-women contacts, and the increase of leisure. The Christian has always had a difficult time writing an ethic for affluence. And the problem of monetary affluence in America can be compared to sexual affluence."[2] The two are essentially similar: each is a matter of big-time having.

This bracketing of sex with the other consumer-goods of affluence is taken for granted by *Playboy*, a periodical which (along with its competitors) is read very widely indeed. It speaks both verbally and visually about Venus in its own preferred version but about other things as well: "The good life is good sex, good food, good wine, good clothes, good settings, and so forth. In the affluent society . . . enjoying life can be achieved by improved techniques, and *Playboy* is the monthly correspondence course in technique."[3] In a book which tells us much about that monthly and its famous founder, a recent writer speaks frankly of America's "expanding erotic consumerism",[4] this being his principal theme: he tries bravely to represent it as a healthy development, but with little success. For the most part, his exhaustively

[2] Rustum and Della Roy, *Honest Sex* (London: George Allen and Unwin, 1969), 49. When this book was published, the hope of ever-expanding affluence seemed more plausible than it has since become.

[3] Ibid., 29.

[4] Gay Talese, *Thy Neighbour's Wife* (London: Collins, 1980), 524.

detailed and realistic picture shows us only the spectacle of extremely limited people attempting to enact earthily Dionysiac roles that are simply too big for them. The attempt does not seem to make them very happy.

For my part, I enjoy the trivial pleasures of affluent consumerism—when they come my way—very much indeed: probably more than is good for me. Nobody has a keener relish for the big steak, the very dry martini, the intercontinental jet, the Grand Babylon Hotel, and all similar delights: they are profane but not usually wicked until we start *requiring* them. But it's the pagan in me, rather than the Catholic, who is disconcerted and saddened to see the Great Goddess, the Earth-Mother, reduced to such company and included among the petty things which we desire to possess and consume, and even—absurdly—among the things we *need*.

This last point deserves some emphasis. Among the characteristics of our present culture, Margaret Mead noticed an "insistence upon a continuous sex life throughout life as something as necessary as digestion—and indeed very like it".[5] The two things are very different in fact. People have real needs, and a workable digestion is among these, as is something to eat and digest from time to time: many people have the former but not enough of the latter, this world being full of actual malnutrition, actual starvation. We might not be able to do very much about this, even if we tried harder than we do. But there is an ugly flippancy in the prediction once made by an influential prophet of sexual consumerism, that "We may eventually come to realise that chastity is

[5] Margaret Mead, *Male and Female* (London: Pelican Books, 1962), 13.

no more a virtue than malnutrition."[6] You do not die abjectly when denied regular and satisfactory orgasm: you do not even break out in spots or neuroses. We have our sexual instincts and desires, greater or less in their felt intensity and possibly departing in some degree from the normal: society has its sexual customs, and we shall be under social pressure to conform to the pattern currently taken by these. There is also a social need for babies if life is to carry on. But in no further sense does any individual have any sexual *needs* at all.

That may seem a provocative assertion. I always find that it arouses a storm of angry contradiction, but a storm which almost immediately subsides into uncertainty and then into an astonished kind of agreement. A seeming novelty or paradox of the most outrageous kind is thus—rather traumatically—recognised as an obvious truth.

There is a big difference between a real need and a satisfaction to which one has become habituated. I have heard the individual's 'need' for sexual satisfactions bracketed explicitly with America's 'need' for Middle-Eastern oil. At the time in question, the one was being questioned by the Pope while the other was being endangered by Middle-Eastern politics, to the exactly parallel outrage of the angry speaker. Such impudence! Aren't we entitled to have what we want?

About anything which they still apprehend as sacred, people do not speak in the language of greedy grasping consumerism.

It is certainly convenient for us to cut Venus down to

[6] Dr. Alex Comfort on the B.B.C., 1963, as quoted in Mary Whitehouse, *Whatever Happened to Sex?* (Hove, England: Wayland Publishers, 1977), 16.

size and make her into little more than a consumer-good, a personal entitlement and satisfaction: she is thereby tamed, she becomes more manageable. "Love, above all eros, is by nature something that cannot be fitted smoothly and easily, without problems, into the functional context of utilitarian plans. . . . On the other hand detached sex as a 'consumer good', as a 'ware', can be smoothly installed and planned into the great utilitarian organisation—as has been persuasively described in a number of important literary visions of the future, such as Aldous Huxley's *Brave New World*."[7]

Alternatively or as well, we can cut Venus down into a game, an amusement, a sport.

There is certainly an element of play in normal happy love-making, in the animals and in ourselves too, and this is as it should be. Venus is still "laughter-loving", and however sacred she may be, she is not God and must not be taken too seriously. "Indeed we can't be totally serious without doing violence to our humanity. It is not for nothing that every language and literature in the world is full of jokes about sex. Many of them may be dull or disgusting and nearly all of them are old. . . . The mass of the people are perfectly right in their conviction that Venus is a partly comic spirit. We are under no obligation at all to sing all our love-duets in the throbbing, world-without-end, heart-breaking manner of Tristan and Isolde: let us often sing like Papageno and Papagena instead."[8]

But while it's one thing to recognise that the proper

[7] Josef Pieper, *About Love* (Chicago: Franciscan Herald Press, 1974), 110.

[8] Lewis, *Four Loves*, 114–15. Lewis may or may not have intended an allusion to that tuneful couple's notion of 'family planning'.

service of Venus includes a playful and even comic
element, it's something quite different to reduce that
service itself to a game and no more.

A game may be defined as an activity that serves no
purposes and has no consequences outside itself; and in
that sense, a totally 'pure' game probably cannot exist in
the concrete. Even chess has its consequences: it helps
you to relax, and it may fill you with the joy of victory or
the bitterness of defeat, so affecting your mood and your
behaviour for the rest of the day. Professional sport is
very far from that 'purity': it has become Big Business in
one way and ritualised tribal warfare in another, and
there are some for whom it is a kind of religion. But
some of our petty and private amusements do qualify,
up to a point; and once contraception has eliminated its
biological purpose and its most obvious consequence,
casual love-making can perhaps be included among
these. It is, after all, fun.

But will it *remain* fun? The danger is that in this area
also, to eliminate sacredness is to eliminate meaning; and
anything petty and meaningless can soon become the
most tremendous bore. "Those who subscribe to the
'sex as fun' thesis or who, like Alex Comfort, regard it as
the most important human sport, also think of it in some
way as an end in itself. The trouble is that when sex
becomes fun and nothing else, it generally ceases to be
fun; the playmate becomes a plaything; the element of
lightness and joy goes out of it; it becomes sick."[9]
For some young citizens of the permissive society, we
are told, "what used to be called love-making" is now
experienced as so futile "that they tell us it is hard

[9] Joseph Blenkinsopp, *Sexuality and the Christian Tradition* (London: Sheed and Ward Stagbooks, 1970), 102.

for them to understand what the poets were talking about".[10] Few therapists find them sexually repressed nowadays. "But what our patients do complain of is lack of feeling and passion. 'The curious thing about this ferment of discussion is how little anyone seems to be enjoying emancipation.' So much sex and so little meaning or even fun in it!"[11] Thus we find students —apparently representative—reported as taking to drugs because sex was so boring:[12] thus we find one girl explaining her promiscuity by the fact that "It's just too much trouble to say no."[13]

In an essentially trivial matter, why should one bother to say No *or* Yes?

It may well be that today's 'permissiveness' carried within it a backlash of boredom and indifference from the very start. It is in no very recent book that we read these words: "Social confusion has now reached a point at which the pursuit of immorality turns out to be more exhausting than compliance with the old moral codes."[14] As to the present-day prevalence of that disillusioned backlash, we clearly cannot be sure. It will only be the really bad cases that come to the therapist's attention, and there will doubtlessly be some who assure us—perhaps on the basis of much personal experience— that the game of sex-as-fun, if played sensibly, can remain fun and never become tedious at all. But such testimony must always be open to doubt. People are seldom candid about the failure of anything in which they have placed great hopes, especially when some

[10] May, *Love and Will*, 60.
[11] Ibid., 40.
[12] Ibid., 60.
[13] Ibid., 120.
[14] De Rougemont, *Passion and Society*, 25.

personal failure of their own may be responsible. We are all under heavy pressure to be, or at least to seem, great achievers in all that we undertake; and for the young male especially, sexual achievement is a matter of crucial sensitivity. He can abstain without creating problems for himself. But if he tries and fails, his whole sense of maleness and identity is going to be undermined; and it very frequently is, as all the campus therapists report.

At the best, and quite apart from any moral considerations, the game of sex-as-fun is a precarious one. It includes elements of both technique and competition, and is threatened by failure as well as by boredom. Margaret Mead saw 'dating', as practised in the American 1940s, as an essentially competitive activity, having little to do with love or even with desire, the ideal end-product being nothing more than a visible proof of the boy's popularity, his social success, his achievement in a competitive field.[15] Sex-as-fun is open to the same danger except where wholly personal and private and sometimes even there: it is a field of achievement and you therefore need to know the techniques, a fact of great benefit to some publishers. "Copulation-centred thought about human sexuality seeks, in the name of liberation, to turn us into sexual virtuosos. 'So and so', we hear people say, 'is good in bed'. Skill in love-making is extremely important to acquire, but when we make it an end in itself and remove the spiritual and total commitment aspects, we relegate sex to the same level as 'she plays a good hand of bridge' or 'he plays a good round of golf'. It belongs to a totally different under-

---

[15] See Mead, *Male and Female*, especially Ch. 14.

standing of what life is all about"[16]—certainly not to the "understanding" that we found in the temple of Aphrodite and in all those archaic vegetation-cults and fertility-rites.

The great danger is anxiety, which spoils any kind of fun. "When the question is simply how you can perform, your own sense of adequacy and self-esteem is called immediately in question, and the whole weight of the encounter is shifted inward to how you can meet the test."[17] Venus always filled people with fear, in the sense of metaphysical dread: when cut down from a goddess into a game, she can fill us with anxiety instead, and perhaps especially if we live in so achievement-oriented and technological a society as that of the United States. Again and again, while waiting at American airports, I have found myself marvelling at the many paperbacks that were there on display—the ones which, being about the game of sex, said in one way or another "You too can be a great achiever!"—with the implication that in so very competitive and exacting a field you probably won't, or not unless you buy this book and master the techniques by assiduous study and practice, never letting up for one moment.

Such books sell widely. It is sad to reflect upon the anxieties thus intensified for commercial exploitation. They might be better reserved for bridge and golf.

It is always rash to cut the ancient gods down to size. They have psychological and other ways of being revenged for such impiety.

[16] Gavin Reid, *The Elaborate Funeral* (London: Hodder and Stoughton, 1972), 109.
[17] May, *Love and Will*, 41.

Our present instinct to cut Venus down to size finds many different kinds of expression: the problem is that of finding any clear manifestation of a contrary instinct. There is no difficulty in finding instances of her de-sacralisation.

One such instance does call for mention. I venture with much trepidation into the field of feminism and Women's Lib: its air whistles with too many bullets for my comfort. Many aspects of that cause are admirable beyond all doubt. But others are more questionable; and there is a certain sense in which, when we work for unqualified 'equality' between the sexes, we are trying to reduce the overall area within which one's physical sexuality is going to be seen as an important thing. Its importance is irreducible and inescapable, of course, in the limited area of reproduction: when it comes to the begetting and bearing and feeding of a baby, the differences between men and women are not to be denied. But are they of no wider importance? Is not Venus a great goddess in any more universal sense, having her relevance to the whole of life? If we set narrow limits to her importance, we shall undoubtedly be cutting her down to size. This is done, for example, by those who now desire to see women ordained as Catholic priests.

I myself take this aspiration to be an absurd one, so far as any full sacramental and sacrificial notion of priesthood is concerned. The word does have a wider sense, of course, as referring to any general office of leadership in religious instruction and prayer; and in this wider sense, the work of Catholic 'priesthood' is already in female hands for the most part. Ask any Catholic where he first learned the rudiments of the Faith and who first taught him to pray: he will almost invariably reply that for him and at the most crucial rock-bottom level, this priestly work was done by his mother in the first instance, and then by the sisters at the parochial school. But things get more complicated when we turn to the more developed senses of 'priesthood'. In Chapter III, I hinted at certain very deep and subtle connections between sex and religion; and it is my belief that if these were worked out, they would explain the Church's instinct to see the sacrificial priesthood as an essentially male thing, so that 'a woman priest' becomes as contradictory a notion as 'a pregnant man'. This involves no belittlement of the female, any more than my own masculinity is belittled by the fact that I cannot bear children. In neither case is there a real grievance.

But for my present purposes, I would lay emphasis upon a far more obvious and superficial aspect of the present agitation for women as priests. It implies that over the large and important area of life known as the Christian ministry, the individual's sexuality should now be seen as a simple irrelevance. Venus is to be put in her place: she has no importance there.

Those who still revere the gods have no desire to cut down their importance.

This desacralisation of Venus finds further expression at the level of sexual morality.

In the previous chapter, I mentioned the curious fact that it isn't only materialists who want to minimise or eliminate all notions of the sacred: it's certain Christians as well, including some well-known theologians. This remains true when we turn from sacredness in general to the particular sacredness of Venus: here also we find Christians, theologians included, desiring our physical sexuality to be seen as a profane thing, of little religious importance if any, so that its handling becomes hardly more than a matter of personal preference. A few of them express this desire frankly, almost in those words. But the majority only do so by omission. They set out to consider the question of what we 'should' or 'should not' do about sexuality; and having given much thoughtful attention to fulfilment and relationship and responsibility, they suppose themselves to have covered the *entire* ground. The idea that we might have some duty of *pietas* towards Venus herself, of religious concern for what happens physically, is passed over in silence.

The illustration of this tendency is an extremely easy matter: one faces an *embarras de richesse*. I shall therefore choose a few instances of it more or less at random, so as to illustrate what I have in mind. The reader may perhaps accuse me of labouring the factually obvious, of simply fixing a new and adversative label upon something universally recognised and mostly welcomed as a kind of liberation—as a shift of emphasis from law to love, from the narrowly biological to the fully personal, from neurotic distrust to joyful acceptance. If so, I beg his pardon for labouring the obvious but not for questioning that optimistic diagnosis of it.

This development is at its clearest, as one might expect, in those writers who are most ethical but least religious. "In order to clear the field of thought so that new ideas can take root and grow, it is necessary to be certain what of the old mental prepossessions will have to go. We must wrench our minds from the domination of religion over sexual matters."[18] In those

[18] Dr. Helena Wright, *Sex and Society* (London: George Allen and Unwin, 1968), 82.

words, which come from a very influential work, we see no explicit rejection of religion as such, but only a dogmatic assertion that it must be kept separate and distinct from sexuality. We might therefore expect the writer to be frankly and fully 'permissive', and so in a sense she is. But only in one sense: in another, she is firmly and sternly moralistic. Elsewhere in the same book, she is as hard on prostitution as any Christian could be, calling it an "exploitation of human emotions" and "the lowest form of degradation";[19] and she goes so far as to propose a NEW CODE OF SEXUAL BEHAVIOUR (so headed in capitals), warning us that it will "be more difficult to follow, and demand higher standards of behaviour than those [codes] which are at present tolerated"[20] and will call for "great stability of character".[21] Her code is a short one: it consists of seven sentences, each of which contains either a "should" or a "must".[22] This hardly sounds like the language of any do-as-you-like permissiveness.

But this author's moralism, although severe and exacting in its way, is highly selective. It is *wholly* concerned with what happens psychologically and in terms of personal relationships: there is no suggestion in her book that sexual acts of the physical or bodily sort are—in themselves—of any importance at all. We have seen that the evil of prostitution is, for her, extreme. But it resides in the commercial relationship, not in the thing done, and her judgment upon it might be deemed arbitrary. If we share her moral neutrality about sexual

[19] Ibid., 113.
[20] Ibid., 90.
[21] Ibid., 92.
[22] Ibid., 91.

acts, what is so degrading about this kind of demand being met by this kind of supply, on mutually acceptable terms? Why should a brothel, if well conducted, be more of an "exploitation" than a restaurant? In each, you pay to have a bodily appetite agreeably satisfied by the services of others.

I dwell upon this author because she offers so perfect an example of what I mean by the desacralisation of Venus. Her position, which is shared by many, could in fact be summed up in three dogmatic assertions. (a) Sexuality is—or should be—a subject wholly unrelated to religion: it has nothing to do with any possible God or gods. (b) Our sexual behaviour must however be governed by a rigorous moral code. (c) But this code does not cover bodily actions, which are of little or no moral importance in themselves: it concerns psychology, personal development, and human relations alone.

Sometimes explicitly and sometimes not, those three principles govern a very large proportion of present-day thinking about sexuality, and not only among materialists and post-Christians.

The writer just quoted is much concerned with ethics, but would not (I believe) describe herself as a Christian. Among those who do so describe themselves, attitudes vary. There are some clergymen who attain notoriety by going all the way down *Playboy* Road, as though joyously and without misgivings. But there are a much larger number who, although unwilling to follow that road to its end, are made uneasy by the question of where they ought to stop, and why. The old morality (they feel) is no longer meaningful and relevant. But what is to replace it, if not simple libertinage? In practice, they commonly replace it with a thinly Christianised version of the three dogmas just set forth.

So, for example, with two high-minded Christians whose permissiveness is far from complete. "Instead of being the first question of sex ethics, whether or not coitus has occurred should be the last. Pre-marital coitus may or may not be a sin, but absence of love always is."[23] And again: "It is important not to ask whether coitus has occurred: it is important to avoid words such as *adultery*. The important question is: Were relations deepened so as to make all the persons concerned more able to become whole, to give to others, and so on? We foresee an inevitable and rapid increase in such co-marital relationships and regard it as the Church's urgent business to provide guidelines for the most creative conduct within them."[24] And again: "The Christian believes that he has most important things to say about relationships and that he speaks about sexuality and its expression primarily as it relates to deepening or preserving relationships. Hopefully, the Church will play down the relative importance of sexual behaviour to which it attached far too much significance for our present day."[25]

We find an exactly similar tendency among Catholics —that is to say, among those Catholics who are in some degree of conflict with the tradition and authority of their Church. Within my hearing, a certain priest once

[23] Roy, *Honest Sex*, 87–88.

[24] Ibid., 107–8. Note that "the Church" is there conceived in broad and mostly Protestant terms.

[25] Ibid., 186. Clearly enough, it is physically sexual behaviour that the authors have in mind.

cried out as though in exasperation: "For pity's sake, let's keep the Church out of the bedroom!" He was not recommending universal celibacy, even though the Church does consist mostly of married people whom the bedroom sometimes attracts, not only for sleeping purposes. It was the teaching Church that he had in mind, Popes and bishops and priests above all: he meant that such people should keep their celibate noses out of the nuptial chamber, refraining from priestly comment upon what went on within it. But by implication and no doubt unconsciously, he was fairly and squarely denying Venus her divinity. Priests, by definition, are men professionally concerned with the sacred: it's their business, whereas the profane is not. You define anything as profane when you declare it to be no business of the clergy.

Another Catholic priest, a writer this time, is more explicit: for him, the desacralisation of Venus is something frankly desirable, nobly attempted in Old Testament times but not fully accomplished even in our day. He claims to have shown "that in breaking away from the mythical world of meaning, the worshipers of Yahweh cleared the way for a genuinely human understanding of the erotic and its role in society. Also, that their history shows the difficulty of maintaining a truly human and personal holding-point at the center of the many tensions built into sexuality." Very pointedly, he then goes on to say "To have desacralised and demystified sexuality was in itself no mean feat; after all, *we still have the same task to perform today* in a culture so vastly different from that of the ancient Near East."[26]

[26] Blenkinsopp, *Sexuality*, 35: emphasis added.

Similarly, a few pages later: "The demythologising and desacralising of sexuality cannot be achieved once for all but has to be fought for all the time."[27]

With some variety in detail and emphasis, this desacralising of Venus characterises a whole and influential school of present-day Catholic thinking, in marked contrast with what was traditionally believed and said. Thus one writer—a psychiatrist, widely regarded as a leader or prophet in the field—tells us that "The shift from biology and physiology to person and love is a good beginning for the mammoth task ahead and one which is in keeping with the theology of Vatican II."[28] The last ten words amount to little more than a ritual incantation and can safely be ignored: in certain semi-Catholic circles, it has long been customary to claim the backing of the Second Vatican Council, no matter how arbitrarily, for one's own ideas about how Catholicism ought to be modified. But the proposed "shift" or modification is clear enough. This "new sexual ethic" will involve no *pietas* towards Venus, no suggestion that bodily actions might have religious momentousness in themselves: it will be a matter of personal and interpersonal development alone. "A sexual morality is outlined which has as its basis the concept of person, in terms of human wholeness, and love, conceived in terms of an ideal which seeks in sexual expression to involve as much of oneself and to interact with as much of the whole person of the other as is possible. The traditional con-

[27] Ibid., 40.
[28] Jack Dominian, *Proposals for a New Sexual Ethic* (London: Darton, Longman and Todd, 1977), 25.

cepts of permanency, faithfulness, creativity and life are expressed *anew* in psychological terms of interaction between persons expressing authentic love."[29]

It is perhaps natural that a psychiatrist should emphasise the psychological: a Christian should hardly give it so total a primacy.

In themselves, these few instances prove nothing. But they are not meant to prove anything. Their function is purely illustrative: they are meant to draw the reader's attention to a tendency which will already have come before him if he reads the relevant books or listens to the relevant sort of conversation. The fact of that tendency is hardly in dispute: the question concerns its interpretation.

I would call it a healthy tendency as regards its positive side, in respect of what it emphasises. There is much to suggest that in the Christian past, too many people assumed that physical actions and formally-defined relationships were the *only* thing that mattered. Your proposed sexual behaviour cannot be labelled as fornication, or adultery, or perversion? It will not be falsified by contraception? In that case it's all right: go ahead!

It will not necessarily be all right; and if we are now being reminded of the fact, that is all to the good. Your proposed or possible sexual behaviour, although deserving no label of that sort, may yet be thoroughly selfish and inconsiderate; it may be such as to generate stress and hatred and misery within your marriage, rather than peace and love and happiness; it may involve a brutal using of the other party, as a mere means to your

[29] Ibid., 10.

own satisfaction. The ugly possibilities are many, but so are the good and happy possibilities. It follows that *pietas* towards Venus is not the only thing that we need to care about when in bed with somebody else or in the whole wider relationship of sex. The 'love of neighbour' is very much involved.

It does not follow, however, that such *pietas* must now become a thing of no importance—that Venus should now be seen in profane terms alone, that the physical is of little or no religious significance, that the love of God has no direct implications for *matrimonium*.

Under that negative aspect, the tendency in question is—I suggest—irreligious and subtly unrealistic too. In the metaphorically pagan language which I have been using, it is irreligious—dangerous too—in that it involves the belittlement of a great and powerful goddess: in more Christian terms, its implications are clearly Manichaean, as is every exaltation of the psychological or spiritual at the expense of the bodily. Its lack of realism becomes most clearly apparent in a distinctive kind of linguistic falsity. The desacralisers of Venus would doubtlessly prefer to be called prophets of love: either way, they seem unable to state their case except in an excruciatingly flatulent sort of jargon, such as must always arouse the distrust of a sensitive reader.

We have just seen a few mild instances of this. The important thing, we read, is for "relations" to be "deepened" so that people can be "more able to become whole"; sexuality has its "expression", and this relates to "deepening or preserving relationships". What Christians must find and maintain is "a truly human and personal holding-point", and what they must value is "human wholeness", in the pursuit of which they must "involve" and "interact". But this is relatively mild stuff, hardly qualifying—as such jargon often does elsewhere, and most richly—for inclusion in Pseuds' Corner. In more extreme cases, we constantly read of how—by means of their caring and compassionate love-lives—people are to 'fulfil their potential' and so become 'truly persons' and 'more fully human' and of course 'mature', while the dreaded spectre of 'meaningful' haunts the murky scene.

Such abuses of language—they have certain roots in existentialist philosophy, and others in the windier reaches of the social sciences—must always inspire distrust. One sees vaguely what the authors were, vaguely, getting at. But one gets an overwhelming impression that if their message were put into less inflationary language—into simpler terms of being good, of being happy, of being kind, even of keeping one's promises—it would turn out to be less grandly portentous than they want it to seem.

As a professional critic, I would beg such writers to be more careful. Jargon is what people use for plugging the holes in their thought: where there is a great deal of jargon, we naturally suspect a great paucity of thought, a suggestion of meaning where there is little or none. It would be useful for them to remember, for example, that nobody can ever become 'more truly a person' or 'more fully human'. I have always been truly a person and one hundred per cent human, as were St. Francis of Assisi and Adolf Hitler. As for our 'potential', some of it is best unfulfilled, as was my childhood potential of becoming a mass-murderer. Those who are Christians might also remember the words of Jesus, who did not say "Unless you become mature and fully human persons, you shall not enter into the Kingdom": in fact, his attitude towards every possible notion of this-worldly development and fulfilment and satisfaction appears to have been sadly negative.

I seldom find myself in agreement with Dr. Alex Comfort, whom I have quoted once or twice already: he is an agreeably ribald writer but an extreme trivialiser of Venus. But I do sympathise when he pours scorn upon those of his medical colleagues and others who wag cautionary fingers at the dangers of 'immaturity' in sexual relationships: on such lips, theirs is just the vestigial but continuing voice of priestly moralism, "the final squeal of the bagpipe after the full-throated organ-playing of earlier experts".[30]

The kind of jargon that I have in mind has one particular drawback: it makes the whole business of sex seem absurdly ethereal, so suggesting that the writer hasn't really got his eye on the object—as when copulation (a very functional and down-to-earth affair) is said to be a means of 'expression' or 'communication'. Two writers already quoted are uneasily aware of this danger. "Our secular colleagues will no doubt find a lot of this writing about sex as a deep means of communication far too solemn and pretentious."[31] True enough, as in the following splendid instance. "Sex, in the more specific sense, is that feeling response to another person that makes one desire to weld that person's life and one's own into a common life, with a total sharing both bodily and spiritual."[32] That will do well enough as an

[30] Alex Comfort, *The Anxiety Makers* (London: Nelson, 1967), 4.
[31] Roy, *Honest Sex*, 52.
[32] Charles Davis, *Body as Spirit* (London: Hodder and Stoughton, 1976), 134.

account of what 'being in love' feels like, and of how we hope marriage will turn out. But as a definition of (specifically) sex, it is preposterous. There is a better realism in the crudest indecencies of the locker-room and the limerick.

I grew up on a farm, and had sharp inquisitive eyes when young. Those too-earnest, too-lofty idioms make me remember the spectacle of a stallion embarking upon deeply meaningful communication with a mare, or a bull expressing a mature and fully bovine relationship with his chosen cow, thus fulfilling the potential and expanding the consciousness of both parties.

"The higher does not stand without the lower." We are not simply animals, and human sexuality is not simply a performance by humans of animal sexuality. But it has that character initially. Its head can rise into the highest psychological and relational clouds, but its feet need to remain squarely on the biological ground, on our sacred Mother the Earth.

Any attempt to break with the biological roots and say those loftier things in isolation will be Manichaean in principle and an affront to Venus, who deserves no such rudeness. It will also be extremely likely to make us talk nonsense and sound ridiculous.

Chapter Six

The Flight from Sex

The title of this chapter might be deemed a shade para-doxical. Is there really something going on which can be called a 'flight from sex'? Various charges are brought against the distinctive culture and behaviour-patterns of our time, but they are seldom charges of exaggerated chastity, of neurotic prudishness.

Charges in the opposite sense are brought often enough, and with obvious plausibility. The subject seems to have become an obsession. One might say, with jocular exaggeration, that our generation is engaged in a head-long flight from everything *except* sex. "In an amazingly short period following World War I, we shifted from acting as though sex did not exist at all to being obsessed with it. We now placed more emphasis on sex than any society since that of ancient Rome, and some scholars believe that we are more preoccupied with sex than any other people in all of history. Today, far from not talking about sex, we might well seem, to a visitor from Mars dropping into Times Square, to have no other topic of communication."[1]

There has been much comment upon this phenomenon. Its roots lie further back than the 1920s: it can be seen

[1] May, *Love and Will*, 39.

as an over-reaction to that supposedly 'Victorian' convention of treating sex as though it didn't exist. Hence, in a book originally published in 1929, two humorists could tell us—tongues in their respective cheeks—that "Sex is less than fifty years old, yet it has upset the whole Western world",[2] and by reason of what they affected to see as a kind of conspiracy. "Everybody was fitted for it, but there was a lack of general interest. The problem ... was to make sex seem more complex and dangerous. This task was taken up by sociologists, analysts, gynecologists, psychologists, and authors; they approached it with a good deal of scientific knowledge and an immense zeal. They joined forces and made the whole matter of sex complicated beyond the wildest dreams of our fathers. The country became flooded with books. Sex, which had hitherto been a physical expression, became largely mental. The whole order of things changed. To prepare for marriage, young girls no longer assembled a hope chest—they read books on abnormal psychology."[3]

Things have gone a great deal further, of course, since Thurber and his colleague wrote those words more than fifty years ago; and one need imply no acceptance of their jocular conspiracy-theory if one observes that the sex-industry has now become very Big Business indeed, the most profitable 'vested interest' of many. But the demand cannot have been simply created by the supply: there would never have been such a sex-industry if

[2] James Thurber and E. B. White, *Is Sex Necessary?* (London: Hamish Hamilton, 1947), 162.

[3] Ibid., ix–x.

people had not already started to be fascinated and even obsessed by sex, to a new degree and almost in a new way.

There is a kind of official optimism, according to which this and all other aspects of the 'sexual revolution' represent a newly positive and favourable attitude towards Venus: people used to think sex dirty and shameful (it is said) but now we are learning to accept it frankly and joyfully. I take this to be a psychologically simplistic view of the matter. To be fascinated by this or that is one thing, to be simply and warmly in favour of it is another. We are all fascinated by death and disaster, a fact upon which media-people base their concept of the newsworthy; but it is only at certain murky psychological depths, if at all, that we love such things. The members of the John Birch Society, in the United States, talk about Communism all the time and are in that sense fascinated by it, but it would be extravagant to say that they do so because they are all unconsciously in love with it—though such a diagnosis has seemed plausible to me in certain cases.

The sex-obsession of our time is an ambiguous thing: to say the least, it includes an element of impassioned hostility towards Venus.

This was to be expected. In the previous chapter, I suggested various lines along which, when Venus ceases to be a goddess, she can become 'profane' in the sense of becoming a triviality. But the bi-polarity of sacredness means that this was never likely to be the sole outcome of her desacralisation. "Originally and naturally, sexual pleasure was the beautiful, the happy, that which united man with nature in general. When sexual and religious feelings became separated from one another, that which is sexual was forced to become the bad, the infernal, the diabolical."[4] Those are the words of a somewhat questionable writer and were intended in a somewhat questionable sense. But the danger to which they refer is a real one. The gods are not to be cut down to size as easily and briskly and finally as we may like to suppose. If we deny Venus her positive sacredness, she may not consent to be held down in the simply profane status of a consumer-good, an amusement, a satisfaction. Her sacredness is more than likely to strike back, but in its inverted or negative version alone: she may return as a quasi-Satanic power, a threat and even a horror, forcing us to choose between the two primeval responses of fight and flight.

Some of us might profess to see this as an unreal danger. Venus is, or should be and can be, a goddess of delight: a healthy person need have no misgivings about her. It's only when she is falsified by the puritanical guilts and neuroses of Christianity that she can possibly be seen as a threat or horror. So the thing needed is a liberation from those guilts and neuroses.

So it is said, bravely but unrealistically. The fear of sex, as of something daemonic and dangerous, is not a neurosis induced by Christianity: it hangs over all human experience. I mentioned certain expressions of it in Chapters II and V: it constitutes a major problem for the present-day therapist, not only if he works among the young: instances of it recur throughout the fields of anthropology and comparative religion. Margaret Mead

[4] Wilhelm Reich, *The Mass Psychology of Fascism* (New York: Farrar, Straus and Giroux, 1970), 148.

wrote of the Manus people, of the Admiralty Islands near New Guinea, as they were before any Western or Christian influence had come upon them for good or for ill: "No missionary has come to teach them an unknown faith, no trader has torn their lands from them and reduced them to penury."[5] Yet these unspoiled children of nature, as represented by her, seem prudish and puritanical to an almost neurotic degree: "Sex is conceived as something bad, inherently shameful, something to be relegated to the darkness of night";[6] and this was notably true within marriage, to which no version of 'love' had any relevance at all. "The whole picture"—as here represented—"is one of a puritan society, rigidly subduing its sex life to meet supernaturally enforced demands, demands which are closely tied up with its property standards":[7] it is as though we were reading a critical account of life among mercantile Puritans in Victorian England—though with this interesting difference, that Manus children were reared on extraordinarily permissive lines in all non-sexual matters. They were under strict rules of modesty as regards excretion: they could do as they pleased otherwise, with no respect or obedience towards their elders, and we are told that this led to a certain poverty of the mind and imagination.

So with another people, in a very different part of the world but equally untouched by Christianity. "Indeed their special terror seems to have been sex. People were brought up with quite an exaggerated sense of modesty. It was considered proper for girls to walk with very

[5] Margaret Mead, *Growing Up in New Guinea* (London: Penguin Books, 1968), 11.
[6] Ibid., 126.
[7] Ibid., 132.

delicate steps, so that their wrap-around skirts should not reveal their knees. But in addition to this, they were not supposed to look up. A well-bred girl always looked down at the ground in case she should be in danger of meeting the eye of some bold young man, and so become filled with unwanted desires. Sex was a trap to them, a rather terrifying necessity which could only be met by an apparatus of magical beliefs and sanctions."[8] Here again, were it not for those wrap-around skirts, we could suppose that we were among prudish Victorians, hag-ridden by the sexual negativism of Christianity. In fact, we are among the pre-Columbian Aztecs.

The truth is that a certain sexual negativism or nervousness comes all too naturally to mankind. Of the Lele people of the Congo, for example, we read that their attitude to sex "was compounded of enjoyment, desire for fertility and recognition of danger",[9] that danger needing to be controlled by complex ritual. So, more forcibly, with the Bemba of what used to be Northern Rhodesia, who behaved "as if they were obsessed by fear of sexual impurity", and had—at the cultural rather than the personal level—a fear of sexual intercourse "which cannot be exaggerated".[10]

Such fearful and otherwise negative attitudes towards sex, especially when normal and consummated, recur also in our Western cultural tradition, and by no means simply as a consequence of Christian influence. Nobody could be loftier and more spiritual about love than Plato,

[8] Burland, *Gods of Mexico*, 122–23.

[9] Mary Douglas, *Purity and Danger* (London: Routledge and Kegan Paul, 1966), 151.

[10] Ibid., 154.

but in the *Symposium*, the Beloved who starts us up that
ladder of perfection is a boy, not a girl; and in the
Phaedrus[11] we find it asserted squarely that the *eros*
which renounces the pleasures of consummation is the
most blessed form of love. Such thinking has been
extremely influential in Western history, and as Denis
de Rougemont has shown, it played a major part in
determining the concept of romantic love that prevailed
among us until very recently and still retains much
power. Doubts have been expressed about the historical
reliability of his *Passion and Society*, but his general thesis
seems philosophically and psychologically sound. Love,
in the high romantic sense that was typified by Tristan
and Isolde, refuses consummation: it desires to be star-
crossed, it seeks frustration and death. The romantic
novel, although less tragic, was mostly preoccupied with
the *obstacles* to love rather than with love as such and in
consummation. It ended, typically, with wedding-bells
—these being similarly implied in the long-drawn-out
kiss (authorised Hayes-Office maximum) that ended
one sort of romantic film. The implication was that
love ceases to be romantically interesting when it finds
consummation in marriage: the counter-romantic novel
about adultery says the same thing from another angle.

There is much scholarly dispute about the exact relationship between this romantic idea of love, the Trouba-
dours, the variously anti-sexual Catharist movements,
and the cult of homosexuality. But some connection
between these things is generally recognised; and the
thing common to all of them is a negative attitude
towards normal, consummated, and fruitful sexuality—

[11] Plato, *Phaedrus*, 256 b.3.

and, not accidentally, a degree of opposition to Catholic Christianity.

Christ tells you to love your neighbour, somebody close at hand, especially if you happen to be married to her. By contrast, romantic love tells you to worship some *princesse lointaine*, hopelessly and from afar. If she ceased to be *lointaine* she would turn out to be just a woman, another human being, however delightful as such; and the whole business would then come down with a bump to that earthiness which is favoured in the Catholic tradition but despised by those who are too lofty, too spiritual.

There is ample Western testimony to the generally regrettable nature of normal consummated sexuality. "Man certainly has no inclination to enjoy his fellow man's flesh," said Kant,[12] "and where that is done, it is more an act of revenge in war than an inclination; but there remains one inclination in man which can be called an appetite and which aims at enjoyment of his fellow man. This is the sexual inclination"; and he adds "This cannot be love, but appetite." So also for Schopenhauer:[13] "The act through which the will affirms itself and through which man comes into being is an act of which all men are ashamed in their innermost heart, which they, therefore, carefully conceal; yes, if they are caught at it, they are frightened, as if they were caught in a crime. It is an act which, on sombre reflection, one usually recalls with repugnance, in a more exalted mood even with abhorrence. . . . A strange sadness and remorse follow the performance of the act, a

---

[12] As quoted in Pieper, *About Love*, 93–94.

[13] *The World as Will and Idea*, as quoted in Karl Stern, *The Flight from Woman* (London: George Allen and Unwin, 1966), 110–11.

remorse which is most keenly felt after the first time, and generally is the clearer the nobler the character of the person."

That sounds like an echo of Sir Thomas Browne's frequently-quoted sigh of regret: "I would be content that we might procreate like trees, without conjunction, or that there were any way to perpetuate the World without this trivial and vulgar way of coition: it is the foolishest act a wise man commits in all his life; nor is there any thing that will more deject his cool'd imagination, when he shall consider what an odd and unworthy piece of folly he hath committed."[14]

And as from behind all such voices, we hear Shakespeare's torment over that "expense of spirit in a waste of shame" which is "lust in action".[15]

Most of us, if asked, would probably claim to be wholly in favour of sex. *"Vive la différence!"* we might cry, perhaps with a lewd *macho* grin to suggest unqualified delights in the past and (with luck) in the future too: lock up your daughters, here I come! (I speak here of male behaviour: I suspect that the ladies might reply to such a question on rather different lines.)

But we would then be putting on something of an act, and not only in respect of the male boastfulness which is decreed by locker-room convention. Simple enthusiasm exists in this field but is far from being the whole story. There is also an aspect or potential within Venus which makes us feel uneasy at least, and to which many respond more strongly, by anything up to horrified revulsion. A

[14] Sir Thomas Browne, *Religio Medici*, pt. 2, sec. 9.
[15] William Shakespeare, *Sonnets*, no. 129.

goddess? It is not only a pathological few to whom she seems more like an enemy, a devil.

Actions speak louder than words. If we want to find out how people really feel about sex, it will not always be very useful to ask them. In such a matter, negative feelings—however powerful they may be—will commonly be regarded as vaguely shameful. The individual will then be reluctant to admit that he has them: he may even repress them into his subconscious and then deny their existence in all sincerity. Male answers to any such question are particularly likely to be falsified by the individual's act, his desired self-image. The thing to do is to observe people's actual treatment of Venus, in so far as this lies open to observation, as private bedroom behaviour does not. How do people treat Venus in their more public capacity? How far do they respond to her as to an enemy, by those two primeval responses of fight and flight?

They do so very considerably. We speak of a 'sexual revolution', leading to a 'permissive society': within the cultural development in question, there are well-publicised elements which can be seen accurately in terms of a war against Venus and a headlong flight from her reality.

The latter of these, the 'flight from sex', is my chief concern in this chapter. But I must pause briefly to consider the sense—seldom recognised, yet obvious as soon as one pauses to think—in which contraception is an act of hostility or violence towards Venus.

It is commonly seen in more positive terms—as a practical necessity, for example, in relation to the concept of over-population, in a single family or a country or the whole world. It can thus be argued that this kind of warfare against Venus amounts to a thoroughly just war, one that needs to be fought. But even if this were to be conceded, it would still remain warfare, a mode of violence; and this kind of argument bears every mark of being a rationalisation. It would be more plausible if the cult of contraception—and a positive cult is what it has now become, as well as a major industry involving big financial interests—had started up in response to demographic and similar fears and (as it were) reluctantly. In fact, it ante-dated those fears considerably. People were already calling most enthusiastically for 'birth control', later for 'family planning', at a time when the 'population problem' meant a dangerously *low* birth-rate.

Their real motivation was of a different kind. We have long tended to see our human role and destiny in terms of 'Man's conquest of Nature', as though Nature were an enemy: a similar and equally Manichaean implication lies behind the technological 'conquest of Venus' that we call contraception. This is a way of treating her natural self as an enemy. We do not seek to modify and control and subdue those whom we love and venerate.[16]

Many people attempt, none the less, to represent contraception in strongly pro-sexual terms. They see that the rewards of physical love go far beyond short-term physical pleasure, and they desire contraception to be seen as a way of making those rewards more freely available, at a slightly increased financial cost but at a sharply reduced cost in stress and burden and—in the

[16] See my book *The Delicate Creation* (Old Greenwich, Conn.: Devin-Adair, 1972).

long term—in money as well. The thing thus implied (they say) is a highly positive assessment of Venus and a desire to extend her joyful reign.

It is clear that loving couples are motivated to make love far more often than they are motivated to have babies. But beyond that obvious fact, would any such optimistic interpretation come naturally to anyone who heard of contraception for the first time and considered it psychologically, in the context of mankind's generally ambiguous feelings about Venus *toute entière*?

My guess is that such an observer, lacking our over-familiarity with the subject and therefore seeing it more objectively, would diagnose it primarily in terms of fear and hostility and violence, a kind of warfare and (in the case of the Pill) a kind of chemical warfare.

The problems of the large family can be real enough, as I know full well. But when invoked in this con-nection, they serve mostly as a *casus belli*, a pretext for initiating hostilities whose real motivation lies far deeper, in that fear and hatred of Venus to which human nature is universally prone.

This (I suggest) is the diagnosis that would seem most obvious to anyone who considered the present-day cult of contraception as from the outside and for the first time. It receives some confirmation from the fact that this active fight is accompanied by various forms of flight. We do our best to conquer and subdue Venus, but we also run away from her; and each of these two negative responses, as to an enemy, is an element within a single cultural development.

If it seems paradoxical to speak of a 'flight from sex', let us speak instead of a flight from sexual reality, a cult of sexual fantasy as being (in many respects) preferable to the real thing.

The evidence of such a flight is all around us, not only on the magazine-racks.

There is a story of some soldiers who, being off duty, decided to leave their base and visit a local bordello or cathouse. One of them refused to go. He said he would rather stay in the barracks and indulge his sexual fantasies in private. His astonished comrades invited him to explain this very unsoldierly preference. "You meet a better class of girl that way," he said.

One sees what he meant; and while he was in a minority on that occasion, he there spoke as a man of our time. People have always had a certain tendency to prefer the ideal—even the imaginary—to the real, but a sexual version of that preference now prevails to a degree that is probably without precedent.

It is understandable enough. Private fantasies, whether sexual or not, provide company and other delights that are just as perfect and paradisal as one's imagination can make them: they exempt one wholly from the problems presented by real people (whether prostitutes or not) in all their tiresome imperfection: they impose no burden of response and responsibility. The soldiers who actually went to that cathouse will doubtless have found satisfaction of their bodily desires, but of little else. Its faculty-members are unlikely to have satisfied their secret dreams of ideal beauty and ideal love. Perhaps with the aid of *Playboy* or something similar, the oddball who stayed behind will have been able to retain and fortify those dreams in all their ideal perfection, untarnished by any bruising contact with reality.

Mankind, especially male mankind, has doubtlessly

been addicted to sexual fantasy at all times. The point is that in so far as we indulge that addiction, we shall be retreating from sexual reality, running away from Venus. In the simplest case, we may of course be seeking the best available substitute for a real Venus who is at present beyond our reach: an isolated or timid or unattractive man will make do with *Playboy* when he would much prefer an actual girl. But not all cases are so simple. If they were, permissiveness and an increased availability of physical sex would lead to a reduced demand for pornographic and other aids to fantasy-sex. But this is not what we observe. In present-day London or New York, it is probably as easy as it has ever been for a man who wants an obliging girl to find one. But the demand for fantasy-sex, in books and magazines and on the stage and screen, is so extraordinary that its satisfaction has become a major industry, still expanding at this time of economic recession and with an enormous turnover despite high prices.

The sad fact is that in certain conditions of the mind, fantasy can seem better than any possible reality, hopeful travelling better than any possible arrival, and notably in this matter of sex. The aim of desire, says a cynical French proverb,[17] is not satisfaction but its own prolongation: satisfaction can seem a let-down, and the soldiers who went to that bordello will probably have tried to avoid this danger by imagining themselves to be in other and distant arms, the arms of their beloved wives and mistresses. Thus can the ideal be retained in imagination while the real is kept at bay; and for some, this will still be necessary when they are with their

[17] Mentioned in May, *Love and Will*, 75.

all-too-real wives and mistresses. It was noticed as early as by Balzac[18] that many a husband can only continue to desire and enjoy his wife by pretending secretly that she is somebody else, and this can also be true on the female side. In how many a bed, at this moment, is *he* fantasising that he's making love with Marilyn Monroe, while *she* fantasises that she's in the powerful arms of Gregory Peck? (I choose these names from the erotic pantheon of an earlier day: the reader may update them at will.)

The fear of Venus, the flight from sexual reality, is a conspicuous thing indeed. The case against *Playboy* and everything similar is that one's attention is thereby fixed, not upon sex, but upon sexual unreality. So far as the observer is concerned, those are not real girls. They are never going to sulk, or answer back rudely, or turn awkwardly recalcitrant in this way or that, and they are not going to make tearful accusations of pregnancy. Their welcoming smiles are fixed forever and are forever false: they are not even shaped like most real girls, since only an exceptionally well-formed few get accepted for the well-paid work of the model, as corresponding to the ideal currently cherished by male fantasy. They are further removed from human reality by the fact that the camera (which always lies, since it abolishes time) isolates them from growth and change: they will never grow older, each will remain fixed eternally at the precise moment of transition from schoolgirl to whore.

"The trouble with girls", observed one cynic, "is that they grow up into women." In so far as that observation touches the male heart with poignancy, it is a heart at

[18] Honoré de Balzac, *Physiologie du Mariage*, 1828.

odds with Venus, with the realities of sexual life in the human body.

Much nonsense is currently talked about the 'acceptance' of sex and the body. Legally and socially speaking, the printed page and the stage and screen now enjoy almost total freedom in sexual representation. But the dominant use made of this new freedom shows us no kind of acceptance but a chronic rejection of the real as such. "The willingness to gaze pleasurably upon the nudes in *Playboy* and to enjoy the sight of shapely girls in bikinis on the beach is no sure sign of the acceptance of the human body. Certainly, the sight of naked female beauty at that fleeting stage when adolescence has just passed into maturity should give pleasure. But . . . to isolate an ideal moment of feminine physical beauty is precisely to abstract. What is then presented as a result of that mental reduction of bodily reality is not a person in the flesh, not even a stranger, not really a human body, but an abstract form, used as device in the solitary fantasies and selfish purposes of an isolated, unrelated self."[19]

Any real 'acceptance' of the body must come to terms with the fact that beauty is not always its most obvious and permanent characteristic. "It is widely supposed that the naked human body is in itself an object upon which the eye dwells with pleasure and which we are glad to see depicted. But anyone who has frequented art schools and seen the shapeless, pitiful model which the students are industriously drawing will know that this is an illusion."[20] As seen objectively and unselectively

[19] Davis, *Body as Spirit*, 37.
[20] Kenneth Clark, *The Nude* (London: Book Club Associates and John Murray, 1956), 3.

at the life-class, or at any bathing beach, or in the crueller near-nudities of hospital experience, the body is frequently fat or otherwise mis-shapen, ill-featured, clumsy, subject to malfunctions that are sometimes visible, and generally ugly; and at the best, its beauty depends upon a certain particular distance of vision. Seen from too far away, human beings are dots or ants of no significance: seen too close up, they become anatomical data alone, strange groupings of pore and spot and bristle. This is why girls invariably shut their eyes while being kissed.

The fantasising cult of ideal beauty can cause the reality of our bodily existence to seem positively unpleasant. We are told of a nudist commune to which the neighbours objected—not simply on grounds of modesty, because its members went naked, but because, being naked, they were not all shapely young women but were (in many cases) "ugly and repulsive".[21]

If 'girlie magazines'—significantly so called—really went in for the acceptance of Venus, a slightly macabre consequence would follow. At present they represent female anatomy in full detail, but only in respect of its copulatory function as conceived by male fantasy. What if they were also to represent it, upon occasion, at the moment of childbirth? The two functions are, after all, not unrelated: each is an aspect of the one Venus. But such a juxtaposition of photographs would not be very popular. That unity of Venus is something which sexual fantasy has no desire to know about.

[21] Davis, *Body as Spirit*, 37.

There is indeed a powerful tendency or instinct in human nature which—if set forth propositionally, as it seldom is—would take this form: "The real is evil: only the ideal, even in the sense of the imaginary, is good". Develop that principle in a religious direction, and you get those varied theologies of the Gnostic, Manichaean, and Catharist sort: develop it in a political direction, and you get the revolutionary Left: enact it in daily life, and you get various patterns of pathological or willed delusion: apply it to Venus, and you get an impassioned flight from sex.

For Christianity, on the other hand, all reality or being is good in itself.

This is perhaps the most fundamental issue dividing the Church from the world, from the distinctively modern world at least, this being characterised by a marked 'flight from reality' in each of those versions, not least in connection with Venus. "Our modern literature, politics, mystiques, our conception of love and of sex are shot through with Catharist trends";[22] and while the hostility to Venus which such trends imply is mostly acted out in fight and flight, it also comes in for a certain amount of sufficiently frank statement.

It is, for example, a dominant theme of what we still call the 'modern' movement in the arts, even though this is getting somewhat elderly by now. As I have observed and as we all know, the verbal and graphic arts of our time are very much concerned with sex —which is nothing new—and have recently come to enjoy a remarkable degree of freedom from legal and social control as regards their treatment of it. One con-

[22] Guitton, *Great Heresies*, 22.

sequence of this is that they can now express real feelings about it, as against the stylised or conventional feelings of an earlier day; and the real feelings so expressed show a consistent tendency to be negative.

I have found this again and again in my work as a literary critic and (specifically) a publisher's reader, an evaluator of new typescripts for possible publication, novels and non-fiction as well. It is perhaps a little unfair to cite the unpublished and unpublishable book as evidence of anything at all, since it is not available for public scrutiny. But there are some ways in which it is more revealing than the masterpiece or best-seller, since while great art can enrich, it can also falsify. I therefore beg the reader to take my word for it that the anti-sexual tendency of so many famous modern books is even more clearly visible in the much larger number of those which never make the grade.

The witness of any novelist, whether published or not, is of course 'skewed'. "Happy the nation that has no history": the troubles of mankind are what makes for a good story, and if this is to feature sex, it will need to feature sexual troubles. Anybody's *totally* happy and carefree love-life—if such a thing can be imagined— would be very boring to read about.

But while the novelist does need to tell a good story, he also needs to express some basic vision of life, one to which his readers can be expected to respond; and where such visions consistently take some particular pattern, the fact will be significant.

As novelists of our time, Normal Mailer and Henry Miller are extremist rather than typical. But their extremism is in a sense followed, more moderately, by a great many; and while Kate Millett's observations upon it are compromised by her own extremism—an almost paranoid extreme of feminist indignation—they are sharply to the point. As she observes, Rojack (the hero of Mailer's novel *An American Dream*) is staged and even celebrated as an enemy of sex, not simply in his capacity as a wife-murderer, but also in his steady preference for sodomy (represented as a death-thing) over normal intercourse (a life-thing).[23] So with Miller, who articulated "the disgust, the contempt, the hostility, the violence, and the sense of filth with which our culture, or more specifically, its masculine sensibility, surrounds sexuality. And women too; for somehow it is women upon whom this onerous burden of sexuality falls."[24]

The fact is that Miller simply hates sex, or at least puts its apprehended hatefulness at the centre of his literary vision. In this, he is only exceptional in his vehemence, his extremism. One can imagine a school of novelists who, given this new freedom of expression, used it to put forward a positive and joyful vision of sexuality —indecently and immorally, no doubt, by Christian standards, and perhaps frivolously by the standards of those who worship the Great Mother, but at least in deeply appreciative love. The extraordinary thing is the rarity of any attempt in that sense. D. H. Lawrence tried bravely, despite his psychological unsuitability for the task, and achieved—at the most—a highly qualified kind of success. "Although [he] lays a good deal of stress on the ancient fertility religions, he says very little about

[23] Kate Millett, *Sexual Politics* (London: Rupert Hart-Davis, 1971), 14–15.
[24] Ibid., 295.

the instinct for procreation. . . . [He does] seriously
underrate the power of parental feeling and the desire
for children; and he seems to have no concrete idea of
the completion of a sex relation in children and the
family. He fought against these things in life, and he
pays the penalty by a yawning incompleteness in his
sexual doctrine. Though he spends a great deal of energy
on the relations between parents and children, it is nearly
always on its [sic] perversions, and there is scarcely an
instance in his novels of normal parental love."[25] This
is a serious weakness in one who sets out to celebrate
the Great Mother. One might diagnose it in terms of
Lawrence failing to see why the deity of love and fertility
has to be female: he always seems to be celebrating
Priapus rather than Venus.

An instinctive revulsion from Venus is as common
among the poets as among the novelists. For the 'modern
movement', if we may still call it that, *The Waste Land* is
certainly a seminal work: and it has been observed that
while Eliot there harps incessantly upon sex, he hasn't a
good thing to say about it. The note thus sounded still
echoes.

It is in the visual arts, perhaps, that the 'flight from
sex' becomes most literally visible as something characteristic of our time. Developments with which we are all
familiar have made erotic art into a respectable subject: it
is studied academically, illustrated books about it are
freely available. I do not propose to say anything for or
against this new situation as such, but only to comment
upon what it brings to our notice. For primitive man
and for many peoples more recently, the function of

[25] Hough, *Dark Sun*, 232.

the erotic—when represented—was chiefly religious or magical or both: it was concerned with fertility and the Great Mother and also with our attainment of transcendental unity. It could also strive, although precariously, to be simply and sensually celebratory. It achieved something of that quality in Japan, although usually with some suggestion and threat of the daemonic: so also, from time to time, in the West. The 'sexual politics' implied in the work of (say) Boucher and Fragonard is questionable indeed: the girls are there seen as the men's pretty playthings. But they are at least seen as pretty, and the implication is that the play will be fun for all concerned.

The erotic art of the twentieth-century West shows us a very different picture. What we find there, for the most part, is a cultivation of the consciously and tormentingly obscene: the female, in her private anatomy and in general, becomes ugly and is seen as a threat and horror rather than as a delight. The exceptions are obvious and include some (but not all) of Picasso's line drawings. But if one leafs through any history of erotic art, the change—occurring around the beginning of this century—strikes one at once. It is obvious that Renoir and Maillol found women lovely, and equally obvious that Schiele and Klimt found them hideous.

Aesthetically speaking, of course, women can be beautiful or hideous, or anything in between, as their good or bad fortune may decree: something similar doubtlessly goes for men, and there has not been any recent change in the probabilities, except in so far as improved nutrition and easier circumstances will have made for better health and therefore—in many cases—for better looks. The seeing eye is what has changed; and in our time, it shows a clear tendency to see ugliness where earlier eyes saw the holy or the beautiful or both.

It might be argued that if Renoir and Maillol loved women, they did so patronisingly, as from an assured position of male superiority and very much as children love luscious candy. The human male has always tended to see the female as a kind of possession, often a literal and legal possession; also, as a domestically useful piece of equipment; above all, as a sensually desirable object, a nice toy to have and play with. If women have come to dislike this view of themselves and of their position and function in life, we can see why. We men have some apologising to do.

But the feminist movement, like all historical movements, is a mixed sort of thing. It is, partly and conspicuously, a response to oppression and a cry for justice and equality. But it also includes an element of negativism about sex itself, and at two levels. In the previous chapter, I mentioned its tendency to trivialise Venus by reducing the area within which sex is to be deemed important. But it includes a further tendency, expressed with varying degrees of frankness, according to which Venus becomes daemonic and not merely profane. Sex itself, not merely the oppressing and exploiting male, is then the enemy.

Many years ago, Simone de Beauvoir wrote what has since become a classic of feminism. Her foreground thesis concerned women's 'liberation', as conceived in Marxist terms. Women have traditionally been to men as the proletarian worker is to the capitalist: he always controlled the money-bags, and it was chiefly for that reason that he could hold her down in subjection and use her for his own purposes. Despite the limitations which the tunnel-vision of Marxism must always impose, this was a more than merely arguable case.

But at many points, Mlle. de Beauvoir went much further than that. She did not merely accuse the oppressing and exploiting human male: she also accused Nature or Evolution or God, or whatever power was responsible for the injustice of making people female *at all*. For her, quite apart from any more particular injustice, it is a simple "misfortune" for a woman to exist as such, and to be "biologically destined for the repetition of life, when even in her own view life does not carry within itself its reasons for being, reasons that are more important than the life itself".[26] Woman "is from the start less favoured by fortune than man";[27] her reproductive function is her personal enemy, her individuality is the helpless victim of the species,[28] pregnancy naturally inspires "revulsion",[29] and while we all share "the primitive misery of being a body",[30] that misery is worse for the female than for the male, and worst of all in menstruation. The burden of motherhood, heavy in itself, is made heavier still by the sexual nature of its initiation. So let us dream of biological parthenogenesis: "perhaps in time the co-operation of the male will become unnecessary in procreation—the answer, it would seem, to many a woman's prayer."[31]

The men might be tempted to reply with various counter-grievances. Theirs is the weaker sex, after all:

[26] De Beauvoir, *The Second Sex*, 96.
[27] Ibid., 704.
[28] Ibid., Pt. 1, Ch. I, passim: see especially pp. 54–55.
[29] Ibid., 178.   [30] Ibid., 380.
[31] Ibid., 41.

boy babies die more easily than girl babies, and you meet many widows for every widower. A neutral judge (could we find one) might decide that the general burden of being human is heavier for the female in the earlier part of life, but for the male after middle age.

But to that cry of pain, as to any other, one must respond with respect and sympathy, while not forgetting that sexuality itself is there seen as the villain of the piece, the fundamentally deplorable thing. Venus is cruel, a devil and no goddess, and all the more daemonic by reason of her injustice, her capriciousness. She afflicts one half of the human race most grievously, and the other half (it is suggested) hardly at all.

Where life in the mammalian body is seen as an evil, we are close in spirit to those Manichaean and Oriental pessimisms that were mentioned earlier, as affecting certain Christian writers almost to the point of heresy. It is an understandable pessimism: the inherent goodness of all being, although asserted in Scripture and the Creeds and central to all Christianity, is a mystery of faith and can sometimes seem an unfathomably dark mystery.

If Venus receives an outstandingly frank denunciation in the passages just quoted, it is because an exceptionally able and candid writer is at work. Similarly anti-sexual sentiments recur throughout the field of feminist thought and writing, although often expressed more cautiously. A well-known psycho-analyst tells us that they are "frequently encountered today in the woman who finds it difficult to accept her womanly role. This is quite independent of the injustices imposed on women in many societies: it is rather an over-valuation of masculine achievement and a debasement of values which one commonly associates with the womanly; a rejection, often unconscious, even of motherhood; an aping of man, associated with an unceasing tone of envy and resentment."[32]

That moderate statement of the case may perhaps be suspect, as coming from a man. But no such charge can be brought against the writer who, speaking of the more extreme proponents of Women's Lib., tells us that they "have a remarkably 'Victorian' attitude to the reproductive system; it must be kept rigidly apart from the purer, higher organs of mind and sensibility. Once again, the reproductive system is nasty, evil, and utterly unimportant—not this time because sex is wicked, but because the reproductive system is a horrid reminder of the fundamental differences between man and woman. The extremists among the Victorians wished they could have reproduction without sex, the extremists among the Women's Lib would like reproduction without women—test tubes have the virtue of not reminding women of their distinctiveness."[33]

This writer is no believer in woman's rightly hierarchical subordination to man. But she does distinguish between emancipation (which seeks equal status for the female role) and liberation (which seeks the elimination of that role). The latter cannot be fully defined in terms of hostility to sex. But it does include a clear element or tendency in that sense, as do 'unisex' styles in clothes and hairdressing and behaviour. The true friends of Venus do not want her brushed aside.

Let me hasten to say that a comparable tendency is

[32] Stern, *Flight from Woman*, 6.

[33] Arianna Stassinopoulos, *The Female Woman* (London: Davis-Poynter, 1973), 30.

visible on the male side. Men seldom fight and reject their masculinity as some women fight and reject their femininity, apart from those few who talk as though homosexuality were a privilege and a glory; nor is contempt for the opposite sex, where it exists, to be equated simply with contempt for sex itself. But the two things are closely related. Venus is a female deity: to despise women is, in a way, to despise her.

Male misogyny is an ancient thing. Few of us, no doubt, would go along with Aristotle and "look upon the female state as being as it were a deformity, though one which occurs in the ordinary course of nature".[34] But we might be equally reluctant to go along with the male Renaissance polymath who took an extreme version of the converse view and commented upon it theologically. "Wishing to take on human nature in its lowest and most abject state, so as the more effectively by this humiliation to expiate the first man's pride of sinning, Jesus Christ chose the male sex as the most despicable, not the female, who is nobler and more regenerate than the male."[35] Few Christians have seen the humility of the Incarnation in precisely those terms; and most of us, if asked seriously, would probably say that neither sex is sweepingly "nobler and more regenerate" than the other.

But we men, when among ourselves and not in the presence of women, do tend to talk about them in the

---

[34] Aristotle, *On the Generation of Animals*, as quoted in Julia O'Faolain and Lauro Martines, eds., *Not in God's Image* (London: Temple Smith, 1973), 120.

[35] Cornelius Agrippa, *De nobilitate et praecellentia foeminei sexus declamatio*, as quoted in O'Faolain and Martines, *Not in God's Image*, 184.

language of jocular belittlement, as though pretty play-things was what they primarily were. This tendency dominates those publications which are aimed at a male readership and of strong sexual orientation. "*Playboy* magazine has its fold-out 'playmate' of the month. The Penthouse Club has its 'Penthouse pets'. These terms put concepts of relationship down to the level of the family dog. Many terms used to describe attractive girls reveal this low-scale relationship factor: 'birds', 'dollies', 'bit of fluff', 'skirt', 'crumpet', 'broads', to mention but a few."[36]

This might be seen as a mere contemptuous trivialisation of the female and therefore of Venus. But it may have deeper roots in fear—not in any simple fear of what the girls may do to us, but in that metaphysical dread, inspired by Venus, which I have mentioned already. It certainly finds a close parallel in another and similarly dehumanising use of language, observable in situations of undisguised hostility—the contemptuous nicknames which soldiers devise in wartime, so as to reduce the enemy to a sub-man, a beast, even a thing. One might hesitate to kill a man like oneself: one might well be afraid of being killed by him. But the required aggressive violence will come more easily if we see him as a mere 'Hun' or 'gook'; and in the same way, we can overlook the humanity of what we see as a mere sex-object, a 'nice bit of goods' of which nobody could be scared. This enemy also will then be so much the more easy to slap down.

The two cases are in fact closely related, the military mind tending strongly towards misogynism, as was

[36] Reid, *The Elaborate Funeral*, 105.

observed by one inmate of a U.S. Marine Corps boot camp. "From the moment one arrives, the drill instructors begin a torrent of misogynistic and anti-individual abuse. The good things are manly and collective: the despicable things are feminine and individual. Virtually every sentence, every description, every lesson embodies this sexual duality, and the female anatomy provides a rich field of metaphor for every degradation."[37]

Every ex-serviceman will have similar memories, and the psycho-analysts will be ready with their comments. We have seen Simone de Beauvior talking as though it were inherently disastrous to be female, so expressing the fear and hatred of Venus in one version: now we are reminded of how easy it is for men also to see the Great Goddess as an enemy, a threat to their masculinity, and not only when they are in uniform. In the pattern of our jokes elsewhere, in our vocabulary of abuse, we men reveal our habitual anxiety before a Power which we know to be greater than our own—a threatening power, even an evil power.

The subject of this chapter is closely related to the subject of the last. That which we trivialise with the greatest determination is that which we hate and fear most deeply.

The dangers of over-generalisation are obvious, and there must be untold millions for whom Venus is neither a triviality nor an enemy—people who remain more or less unaffected by the 'sexual revolution' and the 'permissive society'. My concern is with the nature of

[37] George F. Gilder, *Sexual Suicide* (London: Millington, 1974), 258–59.

that revolution in so far as it has been effective and the nature of the consequent society in so far as it now exists; and what I want to emphasise is the low or negative view of Venus which then prevails.

Does she really deserve such contempt? If not, we may need to attempt some rehabilitation of her divinity, some rediscovery of the old idea that our bodily sexuality needs to be seen primarily in terms of sacredness. It can turn daemonic when abused, as can many other things, but it can never be trivial or profane in itself: it calls for the most cautiously respectful kind of handling. If Venus is indeed a goddess, our primary response to her will need to be a response of homage and *pietas*.

But in what sense can an intellectually responsible person say that she actually *is* a goddess?

Such an assertion will of course be metaphorical, but this matters little: great truths are often best expressed in metaphorical language. The trouble is that lies and deceptions and illusions can sometimes gain much seeming plausibility from that same kind of expression.

We need, therefore, to cast a coldly critical eye upon the possible 'divinity' of 'Venus'. Homage and *pietas* must wait their turn. We must not offer them, whatever our feelings may be, except upon some sufficient basis of fact, of realism. We do not want to worship false gods.

Chapter Seven

Realism and the Sacred

The argument of this book is capable of being stated in general terms. I would not dream of reducing Catholicism to the ranks (so to speak) as though it were nothing more than one religion among many. But I do suggest that our understanding of it can sometimes be heightened by a consideration of 'religion' in the widest possible sense. In particular, if we desire to ease communication between the Church and the world—or even between the Church and its own members—we shall sometimes find it useful to draw upon the language of anthropology and comparative religion. We shall not prove anything thereby. But we may thus make it easier for each party to see what the other is talking about.

Some might disagree. Those who study anthropology and comparative religion are very largely concerned with peoples who are (or were) more or less 'primitive' and pagan as well, or at least not Christian. What relevance can such studies have to modern people or to Catholic Christianity?

Two things need to be remembered in this connection.

In the first place, we are still only men. Within the last two hundred years and especially within my own

183

lifetime, the circumstances of daily life in the more 'developed' countries have changed so dramatically that we can easily suppose ourselves to be in a radically new situation, altogether special and separate from the rest of mankind. We may do well to remember, from time to time, that we still belong to the same species as the Bushmen of the Kalahari, or the aborigines of Arnhem Land, or the Neolithic men who once roamed the Wiltshire hills of my boyhood.

This awareness may perhaps come easier to us than it did to our fathers. There used to be a confident presumption of Western, white-skinned, and modern superiority, so great as to distinguish us absolutely from everybody and everything that could be called 'primitive' or 'savage'. But we are less sure of ourselves nowadays, less ready to look down upon those who have lived more simply. Some of us look up to them instead, uncritically and in a spirit of romantic primitivism, as though there were no value at all in what we call 'civilisation': there are circles and contexts within which that word, once proud, can only be used with apologetic irony. This self-denigratory tendency is understandable but can go too far: I, at least, attach great value to the civilisation of 'Old Western Man',[1] or to what remains of it. But within that civilisation as elsewhere, we are still only men, still stuck in the same old human condition. So far as the great basics are concerned—birth, life, sex, sin, suffering, death, and God—we stand where humanity always stood and are not so special.

It might therefore be argued that in respect of those great basics, we 'civilised' people should be prepared

[1] See Lewis, *De Descriptione Temporum*.

to humble ourselves and learn from the 'primitive' and the 'savage'. The trouble is that in any emphatic recommendation of that kind, there would be an unrealistic element of that romantic primitivism. But we can at least avoid the opposite mistake, and more easily nowadays than in the earlier time of confident white imperialism and the *mission civilisatrice*; and when it comes to those great basics, we should listen to what simpler peoples have said and grant them a vote equal to our own. There, our vastly increased knowledge and power are of scant relevance.

Then, writing as a Catholic, I would suggest that Catholicism has a great deal more in common with paganism than either has in common with the characteristically 'modern' mind.

Until recently, that would have been taken as a very damaging confession. "Just as we thought! We always maintained that yours was a superstitious and irrational faith, congenial enough to ignorant peasants and primitives, but wholly incompatible with a modern scientific outlook; and now you're admitting it!"

But here again, things have changed. That "modern scientific outlook" has lost much of its old Victorian confidence: its connection with 'science', in the sense of verified certainty, has turned out to be very tenuous indeed. The real issue here is not between ignorance or superstition on the one hand and science on the other: it is between a religious and an irreligious orientation of the mind, a holy and a desacralised cosmos, a powerful and a weak concern for sacredness, for God or the gods. "Christians and pagans had much more in common with each other than either has with a post-Christian. The gap between those who worship different gods is not so wide as that between those who worship and those who do not."[2]

Attempts are sometimes made to re-formulate Christianity, even Catholic Christianity, in a genuine 'vernacular'—that is to say, within the language and the conceptual system of the post-religious and characteristically modern mind, as formed within a desacralised cosmos. Such attempts invariably fail. In so far as a message gets across to minds that are fully of that kind, it can only be a desacralised and therefore unreal Christianity. You need to escape from the desacralised cosmos, and from the limitations of its language, before you can begin to see what Christ and the Church are talking about. No pagan or primitive encountered such a necessity, such an arduous problem.

For that reason among others, I see three-quarters of the Church's present-day task in terms of a *praeparatio evangelica*, a preliminary opening-up of communications. Talking to those who lack the relevant "ears to hear", however useful as a bearing of witness and a personal *askesis*, is otherwise a somewhat profitless exercise.

As I explained at the outset,[3] this book is primarily intended to facilitate communication and so promote understanding in an area now marked by mutual bewilderment. Against the background of what has just been said, I therefore offer two practical recommendations.

The first is addressed to those who find themselves baffled and bewildered by what the Catholic Church traditionally says about sex. So long as they see this in

[2] Ibid., 14.
[3] See Introduction, 12.

primarily or exclusively moral terms, as a message about sin, it is bound to seem an arbitrary message in so far as it does not seem simply and clearly anti-sexual, a message about nastiness. For the sake of mere understanding —whether agreement and the 'assent of faith' follow or not—let them try to see it as a message about sacredness; and if necessary, let them go exploring around in the pagan and primitive mind—with such writers as Eliade and Otto for their guides—until the full sense and bi-polarity of that word is alive and present in their minds, as it was in their ancestors' minds. This intellectual and imaginative task may well prove as burdensome as the task of learning a foreign language. But that's what you need to do, if you want to understand anything written in that language.

Then, I am bold enough to offer a complementary recommendation to the Church—to my fellow-Catholics in general, that is, not only to the Pope and bishops. Do you find that your message falls upon deaf ears, especially when it's about sex? If so, do remember that you are addressing a new kind of human being, blind to much that others saw clearly—those early Jews and pagans, for example. A correspondingly new tactic is needed: any message about sacredness needs to be spelled out and underlined as such. You always needed to be clear and emphatic about the daemonic potential of Venus: now, and perhaps for the first time, you need to say that this potential only exists as a corruption of the essentially sacred, that being what needs to be stressed nowadays. Too simple an assertion that 'sex is a good thing' would obviously be misunderstood: you must try to liberate people from the too-simple bi-polarity of good *versus* bad, into the more religious tri-polarity of the sacred, the daemonic, and the profane. Only then will they understand what you were always trying to say.

That amounts to a twofold exercise in mutual interpretation, offered as though from a position of neutrality. I like to think that it may have some usefulness as such.

But it ought to be obvious by now, not only from my sub-title, that I am far from neutral. I am in fact prepared to go out on a limb and invite contradiction. I believe and assert that our physical sexuality is an objectively sacred thing; that we should all see it in that light as a matter of realism; and that we should treat it accordingly as a matter of religious *pietas*, and only then (though still with infinite care) as a matter of personal and social morality.

Such an assertion is open to several objections. Some would consider it a philosophical impropriety—a kind of category-mistake—to speak of any possible 'realism' in such a matter, or of any sacredness being 'objective'. Others might say, on lines already foreshadowed, that any such talk of 'Venus' and 'sacredness' involves a deplorably mythological and pre-scientific use of language, such as cannot be taken seriously in this day and age: others again, that there are strong theological objections to any such attribution of particular and concentrated sacredness. So, on philosophical or scientific or theological grounds or perhaps on all three, my threefold assertion might seem to deserve the most sweeping, out-of-hand, and *a priori* sort of dismissal.

And even if it survived those initial objections, it might still be deemed gratuitous. Does it have any sufficient basis? Let it be conceded that I have said something that *might be* the case: what grounds have I got for saying that it actually *is* the case?

Each of these objections deserves attention. Much will depend upon whether we believe in God or not.

One possible difficulty needs to be by-passed at the outset. I have spoken of 'realism' in connection with the sacredness of sex: I must make it clear that I use the word in an intentionally *naïf* sense. It is a word which philosophers use technically, distinguishing 'realism' from nominalism here and from idealism there, always with a tendency to raise epistemological eyebrows if one speaks too confidently of 'reality'. But I am not considering that range of questions. My concern is with the commonsense kind of 'realism' which the man in the street—and, more subtly, the psychologist—contrasts with self-deception, fantasy, escapism, and every possible kind of misapprehension. The philosopher is fully entitled to question this. But he only does so when on duty. Like the rest of us, he conducts his personal and practical life on the basis that 'reality'—in a sufficient sense—is actually there and can be apprehended in some useful degree by the balanced and attentive mind. 'Realism', as so understood, is a necessary prudence at least, a way of getting through the day without ending up in the prison or the madhouse; and in that same way, we need a practical 'realism' about sacredness and about sex and about any possible relationship between the two. Life has to be lived: its problems cannot be held in suspense until the final resolution of all philosophical debate.

I imply no contempt for that debate. It is a most

necessary thing: in particular, any religion that wants to be taken seriously must be able to stand up to rigorous philosophical scrutiny. Even so, religion—as such—is not primarily addressed to the philosophical organ in man. The priest speaks to philosophers as to others. But like the doctor and the lawyer, he speaks to them primarily as to men, in their personal and human capacity. One needs to be 'realistic' about a symptom or a summons, no matter what philosophical position one holds, and it is in that pre-philosophical sense that I propose a comparable 'realism' about sacredness and sex.

But while I can thus by-pass the subtler meanings of the word, I cannot by-pass the question of whether any such realism is possible. This is in fact a two-stage question. It might be argued, as by an agnostic, that realism about the sacred is unattainable—that we have no sufficient basis for making assertions in such a matter. I shall return to that side of the question later. But as I have already suggested, it might also be argued that such assertions are absurd in principle—that 'sacredness' is a strictly subjective quality, a matter of how we feel and not of how things are. On this reckoning, it would be equally meaningless to assert or to deny that anything actually *was* sacred, as a matter of fact. There would be no possibility of realism in either sense.

This would be one application of a very influential philosophical dogma, widely invoked in connection with value-judgments of every kind, moral judgments included. We habitually talk of XYZ as being good or bad, virtuous or sinful, beautiful or ugly, and perhaps sacred or profane. Grammatically speaking, we are then saying something about XYZ: it is the subject of our sentence, we predicate some quality of it, and (we suppose) with the possibility of being right or wrong. Tremendous arguments do in fact take place, with each side asserting its own rightness and the other side's wrongness about some question of value. But these are pseudo-arguments about unreal questions. Grammatical structures have deceived both sides, concealing the fact that statements of value are simply expressions of the speaker's state of mind, his emotional and other psychological responses to XYZ or whatever it may be. As such, they are doubtlessly authentic: they reveal the speaker's genuine feelings. But those, and those alone, are what they are about. They say nothing that could be either true or false about XYZ itself.

The simplest case is provided by two children who argue about food. One says "Rice pudding is lovely": the other replies "No, you're wrong, rice pudding is *beastly*". Soon the argument becomes a quarrel: each child, in his zeal for the true doctrine of rice pudding, feels like hitting the other. Then along comes their pacifying and logical mother, pointing out that their apparent contradiction is unreal. Despite grammatical appearances, neither is saying anything true or false about rice pudding: each is correctly describing his own feelings about it. Things would be different, of course, if fact instead of value were in question—the possibility, let us say, of rice pudding being poisonous. We could test that, although on somewhat draconian lines, and so attain certainty. There is in fact much reasonably solid certainty about which things are poisonous, and about a great many other factual questions. But about questions of value, objective certainty is not simply difficult to establish: it is a conceptual absurdity. Anyone who calls for 'realism' in such matters is merely asking other people to feel as he does. In practice, he will be asserting his own ego at the expense of theirs.

So, perhaps, with any possible attribution of sacredness. A man tells us that a certain object or place or process 'is' sacred and should be so recognised by one and all, as a matter of 'realism'. But grammar has deceived him too. He is not really saying anything about the object or place or process in question: he is only describing his own responses to it, which are responses of awe, veneration, a certain fear, and controlled or ritual behaviour. These may be peculiar to himself. But it is far more likely that they have been conditioned into him by the social pressures of his upbringing and background, the entire psychological inheritance of his tribe; and such is the innate conservatism of our species that these pressures may still continue at full force, long after the disappearance of the fear and ignorance that generated them in the first place.

Such shared responses can then come to seem like reliable guides to objective truth. "Everybody in our tribe treats XYZ as sacred": from that perfectly sound starting-point, one can move with fatal ease to "All sensible people know that XYZ is sacred", and then to "XYZ *is* sacred, and any failure to see this is a failure in realism and in religious *pietas* too".

In this respect as otherwise, travel may or may not broaden the mind. The discovery that other tribes attribute no sacredness at all to XYZ may only confirm the traveller's worst suspicions. It shows that foreigners —people different from Us—are a deluded and irreligious crowd.

From this extremely influential doctrine, it follows that there are no moral absolutes. In practice, this conclusion is mostly embraced on curiously selective lines. The possibility of objective rights and wrongs is frequently denied in connection with sexual behaviour, by people who take it for granted in connection with Auschwitz and *apartheid*.

We here find ourselves approaching one of philosophy's most heavily-fought battlefields, with shell-craters and skeletons on every side. The different armies have attacked from different quarters: that is to say, the question can be formulated in a number of different ways.

One ancient approach concerns the reference of abstract nouns. If we say that something really *is* good or beautiful, in itself and objectively, we shall at least seem to imply that there really is something called 'goodness' or something called 'beauty'. Well, is there? These are clearly not 'things', in any sense of being physical objects. But what other kind of 'thing'—entity, Being, *idea*—can it possibly be that has an abstract noun for its name? To the question "Is there such a thing as Goodness or Beauty?", Yes and No seem equally intolerable answers. Is it perhaps a pseudo-question, only caused to seem real by the grammatical structure of the Indo-Germanic languages? Is an abstract noun really an adjective, pretending for grammatical reasons to be a noun and therefore the name of a Something? The carnage in this particular trench has been fearful indeed.

I do not propose to fight those ancient battles over again, but only to point out that we can rise some way above them if we believe in God. 'Goodness' and 'Beauty' will then be among *his* possible names, and will so achieve full grammatical respectability as nouns, though as proper rather than as common nouns. The same will be true of the even more abstract word 'Being'. All three, and many others, will be real qualities of the supremely Real; and just as all creation has its share in God's being, although in variously derived and imperfect modes, so also it partakes imperfectly in his goodness and beauty. We often perceive those qualities within it, and our emotional responses to them may then be powerful. But these, in all their subjectivity, will be responses to some actual presence and operation of God.

Mere theism thus means that in principle, some judgments of value can *be* statements of fact. The distinction between the two will not vanish altogether. I reserve the right to dislike rice pudding, and if you prefer cheap Algerian plonk to Romanée Conti, I may deplore your taste but I cannot exactly declare you mistaken. We are always in danger of erecting our personal preferences into Laws of Nature and of God: the word 'Beauty', with its powerful component of subjective aestheticism, will always need particularly careful handling. But if we come to believe in God, we can no longer say that *all* judgments of value are strictly subjective, incapable of being factually true or false. "There is nothing either good or bad, but thinking makes it so": only an atheist can say that and really mean it.

The point is that the existence of God, once conceded, entails the same consequence in respect of sacredness. This also becomes one of his names, the name of a real quality therefore, present in variously imperfect modes throughout his entire creation and perhaps concentrated at certain points within it. We can still use the concept subjectively, saying that a certain place or object or process 'is' sacred for some people though not for others;

and if we are students of comparative religion we shall frequently need to do so. Thus Mecca 'is' a sacred city for the Moslems but not for others; and even within Catholicism, some things 'are' sacred by custom and conventional attribution alone—the 'sacramentals', for example, as distinct from the sacraments.

But when we embark upon a substantively theological enquiry on the premise that God exists, it will make perfect sense to ask whether some place or object or process actually *is* sacred. We may or may not be able to find an answer: the methodology of question-answering, in such a matter, will concern us later. But the question will be a real one, involving no kind of category-mistake so long as God exists.

This becomes clearer as soon as we paraphrase it in the form "In what mode, in what degree is God there present and operative?" The agnostic may be allowed to call that an unanswerable question: in the absence of a revelation, it probably is. But only the atheist will call it a meaningless question.

I do not suppose for a moment that in these few paragraphs, I have given these hoary questions any final resolution. At the best, various difficulties remain. What about abstract nouns of the nastier sort? If 'Goodness' and 'Beauty' and 'Sacredness' are among the names of God, are we to say the same of 'Evil' and 'Ugliness' and 'Profanity'? Or are these among the names of some Satan or Demiurge? If so, we shall be heading for a dualistic universe.

But the ontological standing of evil would require a book to itself, as would even the briefest treatment of the various other approaches to the question. The most I claim is that any full answer to it will lie in the broad area just indicated; and this gets some confirmation from a certain observable consensus among philosophers. Those who deny objectivity to value-judgments of every kind show a clear tendency to be atheists: those who believe in God tend to believe in lesser goods as well, in some understanding of evil, in such rights and wrongs as those of morality, all objective in their degree, not wholly reducible to our own responses and feelings. The two questions naturally go together, or are perhaps two ways of posing the same question. "Is there a God?" is almost synonymous with "Is there such a 'thing' as Goodness?"

It is a question of the highest practical and even political importance. In so far as absolute values are denied, the prospects for our future will be grim indeed. We are already quite defenceless enough before the Hitlers and Stalins of this world, and very largely by reason of that denial. One of its consequences is that the sacred word 'law' comes to mean only 'the arbitrary will of the powerful', a conclusion towards which we have already moved too far. Things are bad enough under any kind of tyranny. But so long as the tyrant retains some faint vestige of a conscience and remembers—however faintly—that there was once talk of a law higher than his own, some spark of hope remains: he may conceivably repent. But where the dominant philosophy is such as to rule out—in principle—the objectivity of any higher law, that poor spark has to die. The tyrant cannot possibly repent: there is no law against which he could be sinning.

It is not only for philosophical and religious reasons that we need to make a stand in this matter.[4]

[4] For a full treatment of this subject in a brief compass, see that crucially important little book by C. S. Lewis, *The Abolition of Man* (London: Geoffrey Bles, 1943).

I therefore suggest that we shall need to be atheists if we are to deny Venus her divinity, sex its sacredness, on *a priori* grounds of the philosophical sort.

From a different angle, however, it might still be argued that 'sacredness' is a pre-scientific and unreal concept, made obsolete by advancing knowledge and power. The word refers to nothing more solid than a fictitious quality, projected by primitive man onto whatever he found mysterious and unmanageable and frightening; and if he responded to any such *mysterium tremendum et fascinans* by rule and ritual and taboo, this was simply because compulsive or obsessive behaviour always helps to ease anxiety, while not being effective or appropriate in any further sense.

That (it might be said) is why we live in such a 'desacralised' world nowadays. We are simply better at understanding and controlling our environment than our primitive forefathers were, it inflicts much less anxiety upon us, and we have so much the less need for rule and ritual and taboo. Death is the great exception: it remains the ultimately mysterious and unmanageable and frightening thing and is therefore—although irrationally—still treated as sacred. But the very nature of this exception underlines the nature of the principle to which it is an exception. There as elsewhere, any supposed apprehension of the sacred is in fact a delusion, bred of ignorance and fear and remediable by knowledge and control.

This may seem a formidable argument, especially if couched in negative terms, as an undermining rather than a refutation. We can all agree that sacredness is a pre-scientific concept, in the sense of having occupied people's attention long before they knew or cared much about what we now call 'science'. But it is clearly not 'unscientific', in the sense of having been proved unreal by experimental or similar methods. It has not suffered the fate of phlogiston and the Ptolemaic spheres, and it can never do so: only a rash controversialist would declare it obsolete on such lines as those. But he might argue, more subtly, that science has shown it up as a wholly gratuitous supposition. If primitive man had somehow been able to live from the start with our knowledge of how the universe works, of how things happen and how they can be controlled, would he ever have entertained that supposition? It seems more likely that no notion of 'sacredness' would ever have entered his head.

So, while increasing knowledge does not exactly prove that to be an unreal quality, it does remove the causes of our ancient belief in it. Any continuing belief in sacredness will then be 'superstitious' in the literal sense: it will be a mere hangover and survival from the days of earlier ignorance, a symptom—perhaps a mildly pathological symptom—of our chronic conservatism and perhaps our romantic primitivism as well.

In reply, we might perhaps question the crucial importance there given to anxiety. This does not always generate a powerful sense of sacredness. In our own time, anxiety-levels can be extremely high among people who still remain thoroughly post-religious and live mentally in a wholly desacralised cosmos. We might also point out that the religious sense—which always involves some apprehension of the sacred—is not in fact any simple function of scientific ignorance and technological weakness. It can be totally absent from the primitive mind[5] and extremely powerful in the scientific mind. But such cases have at least the appearance of being somewhat exceptional, somewhat marginal. The visibly predominant tendency is for scientific and technological development, urban life as well, to correlate strongly with a more or less desacralised view of the cosmos and of life. It is as though the coming of the scientist and the engineer caused the ancient gods to take fright and run away.

On such reductionist lines, it is possible to undermine and eliminate all notions of sacredness, especially where this is conceived as a real quality, residing in this or that, and not as a mere pattern of response. The attempt to do so will probably involve us in a certain amount of psychological stress. "At every stage of religious development man may rebel, if not without violence to his own nature, yet without absurdity. He can close his spiritual eyes against the Numinous, if he is prepared to part company with half the great poets and prophets of his race, with his own childhood, and with the richness and depth of uninhibited experience."[6] Such a sacrifice, although painful, might be precisely what scientific objectivity requires of us. A fully desacralised world may seem a lonely and meaningless place. But if that's the way things are, we need to face the fact.

But any such argument leaves us with a teasing question, especially if we see mankind in simply evolutionary terms and its behaviour in terms of survival-value. How

[5] See Mary Douglas, *Natural Symbols* (London: Barrie and Jenkins, 1973), 36.
[6] Lewis, *Problem of Pain*, 12–13.

are we then to explain humanity's all-but-universal pre-occupation with the supposedly sacred?

This is not the kind of preoccupation which most effectively helps us to survive and reproduce and so pass on our genetic characteristics. Simple fear has a great deal of survival-value, but only in the measure of its brute realism: awe, metaphysical dread, and ritual would appear to have none at all, except in so far as they consolidate tribal unity, a purpose which many other moods and practices could accomplish equally well. Shared danger certainly draws people together; and in some cases, a certain mythologisation of danger will do little harm and may be positively helpful. The dark forest is dangerous, let us say, because it contains poisonous snakes and fierce animals and perhaps human enemies: the belief that it is also an abode of demons will make us all the more anxious to keep away from it. Such a belief may override any misplaced confidence that we have in our ability to cope with snakes and animals and hostile tribes, and it will then have real survival-value. So with thunder and lightning, which we may perhaps see as the anger of the offended gods. If we do, a guilty conscience will make us all the more anxious to avoid those high and exposed places where they strike most frequently.

But religion, at this level, cuts both ways in the matter of survival. If you have a good conscience, having observed the taboos and performed the ritual sacrifices, you may then suppose yourself safer in a thunderstorm than you really are: a certain amulet may protect you from the demons, but it will not otherwise make the dark forest a healthy place. A powerful sense of the sacred or numinous can thus fill you with groundless terrors or else with equally groundless confidence: either way, it distracts you from that harsh empiricism which makes for survival in a tough world.

Religion or a sense of the sacred is one of those human characteristics—conscience, a closely related thing, is another—which are very hard to explain in evolutionary terms. It should have been bred out of us a long time ago. "Either it is a mere twist in the human mind, corresponding to nothing objective and serving no biological function, yet showing no tendency to disappear from that mind at its fullest development in poet, philosopher, or saint; or else it is a direct experience of the really supernatural, to which the name Revelation might properly be given."[7]

The sceptic may reply that it *is* "a mere twist in the human mind", rather like that mere twist in the human body, the vermiform appendix—useless at the best, inflammatory and dangerous at the worst. He may also claim that within the evolutionary process, certain beneficial mutations may carry irrelevant side-effects along with them. The religious sense might stem from one of these: it would then be an unimportant consequence, within ourselves, of something unrelated and perhaps unspecifiable which really does help us to survive.

But this would be a somewhat desperate argument. Religion can hardly be unimportant. In one version or another, it is an extremely powerful determinant of human behaviour: in so far as it is a mere delusion, it must cause behaviour to be unrealistic and unpractical in some degree, inappropriate therefore to our real circum-

[7] Ibid., 8–9.

stances and our real problems. It will cause us to make
ritual sacrifices when we ought to be sharpening our
spears, and our enemies will then rejoice and profit. It
can even make some of us into celibates and martyrs, so
militating in some degree against its own survival. Why
do we bother with anything so unreal, instead of living
sensibly and pragmatically as the animals do?

So long as our terms of reference remain scientific and
evolutionary, the mere existence of religion—and its
stubborn continuance in particular, in a harsh world that
punishes delusion so remorselessly—provides us with a
considerable mystery.

But what if there really is a God, one from whom we
are seriously though not totally alienated by the mere
fact of our fallen humanity?

On that premise though not otherwise, the religious
behaviour of mankind—primitive mankind especially—
ceases to present us with any kind of problem. It's
simply that we are haunted by the memory and even the
half-experience of God and are drawn to him but also
repelled by him, so that with one part of our split minds,
we would like to forget him altogether. But we cannot
really do this: we are inescapably reminded of him by
certain elements in our natural experience, and notably
by those which involve danger and mystery. In themselves, such things are more or less manageable and point
to nothing higher. They form part of all mammalian
experience, and those creatures which remember no
God cope with them perfectly well: your cat tempers
her extreme curiosity with caution, which is why she
lives blissfully and has nine lives. It's only because we
do remember God that we cannot live as sensibly and
blissfully as she does. The dangerous and perplexing side

of experience could not possibly suggest the Numinous, the Sacred, unless something of that sort were already present in our minds although dimly, as an object of anxiety and fear but of fascination too. It is only because we are haunted by a real *mysterium tremendum et fascinans*, however distantly and reluctantly, that fear can become awe and that mystery can take on the quality of sacredness, so modifying our practical responses to life on lines that would seem absurd to anyone not so haunted.

Absurd or irrational behaviour can hardly make for survival. We might argue that if God exists, even the crudest religion will be a practical realism at its own level and will thus have its own kind of survival-value. But the mechanisms by which it could do so effectively are far from obvious. On the other hand, if there is a God who cares for his creation and for ourselves in particular, it follows that our story will not necessarily be determined by evolutionary factors alone, by random mutation and natural selection and nothing else. God's finger may be involved as well or even instead. It is hard to think of anything else that would have kept so unpractical a thing as religion in such very stubborn existence.

On this analysis, our apprehensions of the sacred will naturally be subjective, even though shared on some tribal basis: if one thing reminds us sharply of God when something else does not, the one but not the other will be sacred *for us*, the difference between the two being accidental, a matter of circumstances and psychology. But the existence of an actual God raises a further possibility, one that we have seen already. Present and operative in the whole of his creation, God may choose to have particular concentrations of his presence and operation; and if he does, these will be points at which it will make sense to speak of objective sacredness.

We may or may not be able to identify those points for ourselves: they may escape our notice altogether. At the best, experience and introspection will give us little guidance. Our responses to that which is sacred for us will be indistinguishable from our responses to that which *is* sacred. This is where the religious controversies and even the religious wars begin; and it is why we can often concede good faith to both parties, while not ruling out the possibility that one side might be right and the other side wrong.

It remains for us to consider the sense in which science and technology are responsible for desacralising our world. They have done so (I suggest) not by any kind of proof but only by easing our condition and deflecting our attention. As we gain in knowledge and power and become more thickly insulated from primary experience, we are likely to be reminded of God less forcibly and by fewer things: we shall be enabled to pay less attention to those mysterious ultimates against which primitive man, in his harsher circumstances, was held steadily as against a knife-edge—life and birth and sex as cosmically seen, the strangeness of this universe, our own alienation within it, the entire mystery of being. Social fragmentation, a widespread thing nowadays, will help the consequent desacralisation along: such apprehensions of the sacred as we may have will then be mostly peculiar to ourselves, fortified by little tribal support or none, and therefore easier to dismiss from serious attention. No revelation of the objectively sacred will thereby cease to be valid. But we shall lose certain motivations for caring whether it is valid or not:

forgetting the question, we shall have less interest in any possible answer.

Logically speaking, all contingent being entails the existence of God. But not all experience reminds us of him. If you are healthy and well-fed in some modern city, surrounded by the profane works of man and engaged in some masterful and manipulatory kind of work, it is easy to forget about him altogether, so losing all present consciousness of the sacred.

The thing that will pull you up most sharply and inescapably is—once again—the fact of death.

It is no part of my present purpose to attempt any proof that God exists. But I do want to suggest that belief in him will modify our judgment upon assertions about sacredness, as located here or there and perhaps in our bodily sexuality. Without God, such assertions may well seem philosophically improper, as involving a built-in category-mistake: they may also seem to involve a reversion to pre-scientific and pre-rational modes of thought. But once we concede that God exists, such objections will lose their force.

It will be noticed, however, that I have been smuggling into the argument something beyond God's mere existence: I have mentioned the possibility that as well as pervading all his creation, he may choose to be more intensely present and operative at certain points within it. If he does so choose, these will be points of real sacredness, whether we apprehend them as such or not: the rest of creation will be relatively profane, though in no sense evil.

But to some religious people, including some present-day Christians, all such thinking is intensely uncongenial. How can God—the Universal, the Absolute—be conceived as operating in so very selective and arbitrary a fashion? If we suppose that he does, are we not degrading him to the level of some earthly king who likes to indulge capricious preferences, favouring one person or place more than another?

This is an imaginative rather than an intellectual difficulty, though a real difficulty for some people none the less. But it is only one element within a wider problem, one that arises as soon as we begin to think of God the Creator, even hypothetically. How do we explain the *particularity* of his creation? God is the Absolute, conditioned by nothing outside himself: we imagine him as hanging timelessly in a kind of void, a condition of total symmetry and abstraction. How can such an Absolute make particular decisions or take particular actions of any sort at all? What possible motivations could lie behind such particularities? What can it have been that prompted God to create the giraffe but not (as far as we know) the unicorn, Dr. Johnson but not (in the same sense) Mr. Pickwick? Why is the night sky so untidy? Why are the Amazonian jungles so full of unnecessarily elaborate birds? The possible options before the Creator were presumably infinite: how did God choose between them?

I'm glad that he did: that is to say, the complex particularity and even the arbitrariness of his creation is one of the things that I like about it. Even so, it does baffle the imagination.

A very modest exercise in philosophical and theological analysis will show that if we ask such questions about God's motivations, we shall be asking pseudo-questions. If they seem real to us, this will be because of subconscious anthropomorphism: we shall be projecting on God the human experience of facing options and choosing between them on the basis of one motivation or another. This will not necessarily do a great deal of harm—the Old Testament gives us much positive encouragement to think of God anthropomorphically—but we do need to remember the limitations of all such analogical thinking.

As soon as we try to think more literally, two principles become fairly obvious.

In the first place, when we speak of 'God'—even in the most hypothetical way—we are speaking of a God whose 'motivations' cannot conceivably be understood by ourselves. We can no more hope to see how his mind works (if I may put it like that) than a dog can hope to understand the mathematical activities of its master. (I speak here of our present condition. So far as we know, a dog cannot look forward to an eventual participation in human nature and mathematical understanding.)

Then, if we look at the universe—"the works of Nature, also those little frogs"—while believing in God the Creator, it becomes clear that he did and does make 'choices' of what seem to us the most arbitrary kind. Their basis is an unfathomable mystery: their effects are all around us, within us as well.

There is therefore nothing inherently unlikely in the idea of God making further 'arbitrary choices' in the matter of his own presence and operation, so causing sacredness to exist in real concentrations. As far as we can see, on the very broadest basis of merely theistic religion, this is just the kind of thing that God does.

But has he done so in fact? and where?

I have said, as though dogmatically, that our physical sexuality is a sacred thing in fact: I have also tried to give this assertion some negative justification. So long as we believe in God, there are no good reasons —philosophical, scientific, or in the broadest sense theological—for dismissing it out of hand. Something of that kind might be true.

But *is* it true?

To ask that is, of course, to raise a question of the doctrinal or dogmatic kind, concerning such possible operations of God as lie beyond any kind of direct observation. Our approach to it will depend upon our approach to all other questions of that kind. If we are to be Logical Positivists, we shall regard them all as meaningless: if we are to be agnostics, we shall regard them as real but unanswerable.

I take many such questions, this one included, to be answerable in principle and answered in fact, sufficiently at least, though on lines that will leave much mystery still unexplained—as always in doctrinal matters—with contemplation and love and suffering as our primary roads to its deeper understanding.

I did not attempt to prove the existence of God, and I do not now propose to attempt anything in the way of a general Catholic apologetic. What follows is only an exploration of the pattern which such an apologetic might take if couched in the language of this book—a language that may usefully supplement the more usual language of theology and apologetics, but is certainly not intended to replace it.

We might begin with this observation, that anthropologically and in terms of comparative religion, the sacred is everywhere the concern of some priesthood. When people seek guidance and instruction about anything within that realm, it is to priests of some kind that they turn, as being the experts in that field.

But their prudence in doing so may be questioned. The actual record of humanity's numerous priesthoods is distinctly mixed. Priests, especially high priests, have sometimes been guilty of arrogance and ambition and personal corruption in other versions: they have sometimes exploited their standing and dignity for selfish ends. We might be able to forgive them for all that, if only their guidance and instruction about the sacred could be regarded as realistic and reliable. But as most broadly seen, it is hardly reliable at all—not so much because it is in conflict with experience, as because it is in conflict with itself. Different priesthoods say different things: even within the same cult, individual priests can contradict one another most fiercely. "Who shall decide, when doctors disagree?"

One might conclude that the *expertise* of priests extends, at the most, to sacredness of the subjective and socially conventional kind. About the myths and rituals of their own tribe, they may speak with great profundity. But they can do no more; and the best realism that we can gather from that quarter will be respectfully agnostic, conceding a subjective value to every man's or every tribe's apprehensions but refraining from any more objective assertion. It seems that no initiative on our part can yield harder findings; so 'religion' can only be a matter of how different people see things and respond to them, of how they feel. Priesthoods can minister usefully, but only within that considerable limitation. They must never dogmatise, and we must never assert.

This will strike many people as the only tolerable answer to the religious question. But what if the initiative were to come from God's side? What if the particularity of his action were to include a granting of realism and reliability, however limited in scope, to some particular and definable priesthood? We might then hope for some hard information about his presences and operations, some solid realism in our apprehensions of the sacred.

The end-product of the apologetic task, when conceived in these terms, would naturally need to be defined in terms of faith. But this would be (among other things) faith in a God who, for the sake of self-revelation, provides one recognisable exception to the general unreliability of priesthoods. It would not be a total exception: that is to say, the Catholic priesthood consists of imperfect men, prone to the characteristic faults of priesthoods everywhere, and most reliable about the sacred when consulted in their collective extension through space and time. Individuals among them can be a great deal less reliable, especially when bemused—as many are today—by some temporary fad and fashion of thought. I speak therefore of a priesthood, not of priests; and while this is a priesthood which can find concentration into Pope or Council, it is also diffused among millions whom the anthropologist would not classify as 'priests' in any sense at all.

Thus, with much over-simplification and from a somewhat unusual angle, I approach that familiar concept, the mind and teaching of Christ in his Church. We usually and most necessarily understand that concept in doctrinal terms of faith and morals: I suggest that it can also and usefully be seen in terms of a reliable realism about the actually sacred, a realism towards which primitive and pre-Christian man could only guess and grope and fumble, often profoundly and prophetically, never reliably.

What gets achieved, in Christ and through this priesthood, is the transformation and perfection of 'nature', not its simple replacement. All things thus move towards a consummation of universal sacredness, an eventual elimination of the profane. Even natural religion could see ultimate destiny in those terms. "If it is true . . . that the simplest definition of the sacred remains 'the opposite of the profane', it is also clear . . . that the dialectic of hierophanies tends endlessly to reduce the spheres that are profane and eventually to abolish them. Some of the highest religious experiences identify the sacred with the whole universe. To many a mystic the integrated quality of the cosmos is itself a hierophany."[8] This is more crucially true for Christianity. It always saw the profane or secular as—at the most—something temporary, destined for ultimate sacralisation in Christ. Our present mentality, conditioned as it is by the experience of time and free will, makes it hard for us to imagine what will then become of evil and what is meant by the word 'Hell': our final experience may possibly be rather like that of waking up from a nightmare and finding that the horrors have not merely passed but were never real at all. We shall find out in due course: for the present, it is obvious enough that a very un-Christian and even heretical dualism is invited by any undue emphasis upon

[8] Eliade, *Comparative Religion*, 459.

the difference between the sacred and what is now the profane.

But for the time being, that difference is still with us and needs to be recognised. The nature of a destination is one thing, the conditions of a journey there are something else: there may well be a big difference between what we need to do *in via* and what we expect to find *in patria*. In practice, Christians recognised from the start that the Faith and following of Jesus was a matter of particular and concentrated sacredness—in himself first of all, by virtue of the Incarnation, then in the sign and sacrament which his Church is, and then in its particular actions, notably but not only those that are 'sacraments' in the developed and technical sense. "Not peace but a sword": he came to bring an ultimate unity, but by the way of an initial selection and separation, a marking-off and fencing-in, a sharp distinguishing of his sacred *ecclesia* from the redeemable but still profane world. Historical Christianity certainly did propose to sacralise all things. But it proposed to do so by emphasising the sacred at every point and trying to extend its realm and influence, as when a monk made his entire life liturgical, or when a lay Catholic sacralised his entire day by a 'Morning Offering'. It was always a feeble Christianity that limited itself to acts and occasions of the explicitly religious, even the ecclesiastical kind. The profane is there to be transformed in Christ, to be given the religious importance which it now lacks: it is not there to be ignored.

As I observed in Chapter IV, there are some present-day Christians—influenced perhaps by Bonhoeffer and Cox and Robinson and other such theologians—who have a nominally similar purpose but propose a converse approach to it. In order to effect a sacralisation of all things, they want to see all particular sacredness forgotten or eliminated: they call, therefore, for a desacralised or secular Christianity and—in extreme cases—for a religion without God.

Such hopes seem wholly unrealistic to me. In so far as those people get their way, the practical outcome will not differ from that desired by those who are frankly atheistic, frankly hostile to all religion; and these are the ones who deserve more intellectual respect. If Christianity, as known and practised for nineteen centuries, now turns out to be a delusion, let us recognise the fact and discard it, and perhaps every other kind of religion as well: let us adopt something like an unqualified secular humanism. But it is merely pathetic to talk as though we shall then be discovering the point of *real* Christianity, *real* religion, for the first time. "Many of the most vocal theologians of secularity . . . insist that secularization is a genuinely Christian achievement and the true fulfilment of the Christian *kerygma*";[9] and as one such theologian puts it, "For me, secularization represents the regaining of the sacramental structure of reality".[10] Such talk suggests the self-deception of a defeated army that desperately wants to suppose itself victorious. There were some Frenchmen who, in 1940, saw the Nazi conquest as a liberation of the *real* France.

These secularised 'Christianities' can perhaps be seen in terms of over-reaction to the dangers, of superstition

[9] R. J. Z. Werblowsky, *Beyond Tradition and Modernity* (London: The Athlone Press, 1976), 28.

[10] R. Panikkar, as quoted in ibid, 119. This book can be recommended as a gently ironic study of what happens to religion when it attempts to do without the sacred.

and Pharisaism, that lurk in every intense apprehension of the distinctively sacred: the Lord gave us a sufficient warning against these.

What I would emphasise, in the perspective of this book, is the 'total depravity' which such theologies attribute to practically all religion at practically all times. However strongly sacredness was believed to pervade all things, religious man nearly always saw that it needed to be apprehended in particular concentrations—in signs and sacraments and images, in the Torah or the Koran or the Gospel, in the Holy of Holies or the Kaaba, in sworn priesthoods and holy rites, in hierophanies of every kind. All that amounts to one element within the religious instinct of natural man; and here as elsewhere, the Church saw 'nature' as something that needed to be transformed and perfected, not as something so evil that it needed to be replaced altogether.

If God has indeed given a *charisma* of reliability to one particular priesthood, we shall be able to learn from it and so attain a certain realism about the sacred; and part of what we learn thereby is that in such matters, the instinct of natural man was perfectly sound in itself but needed a great deal of correction in detail as well as transformation in substance. The Church provides us—in fact—with a kind of methodology by which his earlier apprehensions can be put to the test, rather as when scientific hypotheses are put to the test of experiment.

Not all of them survive the test: there are various points at which his feelings of sacredness, although powerful, turn out to be subjective in nature, socially or psychologically conditioned, corresponding to nothing exceptional in the way of a divine presence and operation. He told us, let us say, that certain stones and waters were sacred, perhaps fearsomely so. It now turns out that apart from the general sacredness of all being, they were not; nor was the Moon, despite universal and powerful feelings. Whatever might be said about the expensive frivolity of space-travel, those astronauts who landed on its surface were in no danger of committing the particular sin of sacrilege.

But the divinity of Venus is one of the things that survive this quasi-experimental test. It needed the most radical correction and development, on the lines which I dramatised in Chapter III. But it was true as far as it went.

The witness of the Church, in that sense though seldom expressed in that kind of language, was clear from the start. If the 'divinity' of Venus had not been recognised, if sex had been seen as a profane matter, the Church would simply have treated this as one area in which we can do great good or great harm to ourselves and our neighbours, along with many other such areas: beyond the moral questions so arising, our priesthood would hardly have concerned itself with sexuality at all, any more than with so many other things once revered by paganism. There are sacred buildings and altars in the Christian dispensation, there is holy water, but the Church never had anything particular to say about stones and waters as such: the orb of Diana—"Queen and huntress, chaste and fair"—can still generate the most powerful feelings of quasi-religious awe within us, but Catholic theology never included a doctrinal and moral and liturgical treatise *De Luna*. The Moon was for other people to talk about, perhaps as a dead rock, perhaps as a radiance for lovers and poets. It lay beyond the Church's competence: in no way evil, it was profane.

But the Church saw from the start that physical sexuality lay within its competence and was not profane, and that being of God, it was certainly not evil. It had the terrifyingly double-edged quality of sacredness.

A wider recognition of this, on both sides, would go some way towards easing the mutual bewilderment which I mentioned in the Introduction to this book. It would also explain something otherwise inexplicable— the fact that our Sovereign Pontiff sees fit to pontificate in matters of sex, and the even more mysterious fact that his utterances about it are taken seriously by millions. High priests have no competence to speak of the profane: about the sacred, they will be the ones who speak with authority if anyone does.

This also gives us a useful come-back to one familiar kind of complaint. "But I can't see anything wrong with contraception!"—or with pre-marital or homosexual love-making, or whatever it may be. The correct if gnomic reply is "Perhaps you are looking in the wrong direction."

Given so much, given the continuing if metaphorical divinity of Venus, all the rest follows—if not easily and without some controversy, yet (in a real sense) so naturally that we can here adapt an old expression and speak of the 'natural law', despite screams of scholastic protest. Various questions remain, lying beyond the scope of this book. One concerns the practical details of the extremely cautious handling that this redeemed Venus will obviously need: another concerns the pastoral desirability of emphasising her positive sacredness here, her daemonic potential there. I incline to the view that the first of those two questions has been handled rather better than the second.

No such interpretation of the Church's mind will make the Christian's love-life altogether easy. But nor will anything else: I speak primarily in the hope of easing bewilderment, not of by-passing the unpopular Cross. It was always unpopular; and now that people have come to have such extraordinarily high expectations— as though fulfilment and satisfaction were to be enjoyed at every point as a matter of right, as though fortitude should no longer be required of us by God or man—it is likely to be more unpopular than ever. The Christian and Catholic view of sex is a hard thing to put across nowadays. But then, so is a genuinely Christian and Catholic view of life in general. People don't want to know about it: the seed falls on stony ground. It may find the soil more receptive as times get harder.

But whatever our personal reluctance may be, the main point ought to be clear enough if we have any real feeling for sex and sacredness; and it is upon the Church's witness, endorsing and developing that of the pagans, that I rest my case.

This book will probably strike some readers as a bravely desperate attempt to enlist Venus—of all improbable allies!—in defence of a hidebound Pope and the whole collapsing citadel of traditional Catholic morality in matters of sex.

I shall certainly not object if it has some effectiveness in that sense. But my chief purpose in writing has not been of that kind. For one thing, Pope John Paul II does not seem in the least hidebound to me. Only extreme prejudice could use such a word in connection with one

of the most conspicuously lively and penetrating minds
in present-day philosophy. Then, I see no likelihood of
that citadel collapsing, despite the angry shouts of the
besiegers and some desertions from within. This is a
tough citadel, its survival-value is proven; and in any
case, it is hardly my present concern. I have been talking
mostly about religion and *pietas*, hardly at all about
morality.

My mind works the other way round. I would certainly be glad to see the baptised and risen Venus recognised more widely as a friend and ally of the Pope and
indeed of Christ. But I am even more happy to see so
tough a character as the Pope fighting so gallantly in
defence of her and the integrity of her sacredness.

She needs allies, she needs friends. Only within the
firmly Catholic tradition, it seems, is any consistently
religious and therefore high view taken of her: that is
what makes me spring so chivalrously and piously to her
defence and offer her this act of homage.

Not that I have spoken very much about *her*. I did
not want to make this into a sexy book, and I have
refrained from saying what might be said by way of
more explicit homage to this holy mad Princess of all
that is rosy-nippled or hairy-chested, this Queen of the
Seminal and Amniotic Oceans, of love and beauty and
youth, of skin and body-fluids and explosive spearing,
of the microscopic rape that begins us all and is seen by
nobody, of swelling and agony and blood and babies and
milk, of the fierce togetherness of family. I am not thus
reluctant because I'm prudish, but because words fail
me. The poets have tried often enough. But no language
really suffices for so holy and fearsome a Power, so
shattering a conjunction within us of God's love with

his creativity; or for the impious rashness of fooling around with her.

"Put off thy shoes from off thy feet, for the place whereon thou standest is holy ground."